Accounting
for Marketing

ADVANCED MANAGEMENT AND ACCOUNTING SERIES

Series Editor: David Otley

Other titles in the series

Standard Costing
COLIN DRURY

Transfer Pricing
CLIVE EMMANUEL & MESSAOUD MEHAFDI

Business Unit & Divisional Performance Measurement
MAHMOUD EZZAMEL

Financial Planning Models
G ROLAND KAYE

Overhead Cost
JOHN INNES & FALCONER MITCHELL

Social & Organizational Context of Management Accounting
ANTHONY G PUXTY

Accounting for Marketing

Richard M.S. Wilson

Professor of Business Administration and Financial Management
The Business School
Loughborough University

and Visiting Professor
Sheffield Hallam University

|c| I |m|A|

Published in association with *The Chartered Institute of Management Accountants*

For product information and technology assistance,
contact **emea.info@cengage.com**.

For permission to use material from this text or product,
and for permission queries,
email **clsuk.permissions@cengage.com**.

British Library Cataloguing-in-Publication Data
A catalogue record for this book is available from the
British Library.

ISBN: 978-1-86152-468-3

Cengage Learning EMEA
Cheriton House, North Way, Andover, Hampshire, SP10 5BE,
United Kingdom

Cengage Learning products are represented in Canada by
Nelson Education Ltd.

For your lifelong learning solutions, visit
www.cengage.co.uk

Purchase your next print book, e-book or e-chapter at
www.CengageBrain.com

Printed by Lightning Source, UK

To Professor Kenneth Simmonds of the London Business School for his inspiring initiatives in the field of marketing controllership

and to

Professor Stanley J. Shapiro of Simon Fraser University, Canada, for his sustained commitment to the teaching of marketing controllership.

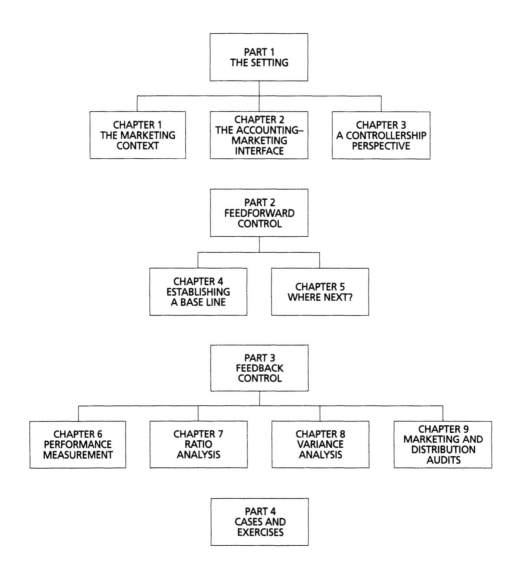

Contents

Figures

Series Editor's Preface

David Otley
KPMG Professor of Accounting
Lancaster University Management School

This text is somewhat different from others in the Advanced Management Accounting and Finance series. Whereas the other volumes are relatively slim, and intended to be used as a small part of a final-year undergraduate programme, this volume is rather larger. The reason is that it fills a very important gap. There are very few texts available which deal with the centrally important topic of accounting for the marketing activities of organizations. In this book, Richard Wilson seeks to redress the balance, and provides a wealth of material that can only be found scattered across a wide range of publications in both the accounting and marketing literatures.

This book will therefore have a variety of uses. It is clearly suitable to be used in conjunction with traditional management accounting texts at final-year undergraduate level, to help compensate for the sad neglect of marketing in such texts. It might also form the basis of a full final-year optional course in accounting for marketing, for those students who have not been exposed to the topic previously. Further, it is also suitable for use on MBA and other postgraduate programmes, and will provide useful material for those whose previous backgrounds have encompassed only accounting or marketing, as well as those who have experienced neither.

Finally, it can also be used to complement texts that concentrate on what has become known as 'strategic management accounting'. Although difficult to define, strategic management accounting seeks to extend the vision of management accountants into the wider, external world in which organizations operate. It considers customers and competitors, future planning as well as control, and focuses upon the value that activities have as well as their cost. However, in dealing with such a wide range of topics, such texts can often deal with accounting for marketing in a perfunctory manner. It is hoped that this extended treatment will add more meat to the bare bones they typically provide.

I believe this text is a most important addition to the series. If it alerts the accountants of the future to the importance of marketing and the ways in which management accounting information can be developed to help analyse and add value to the marketing activity, it will have achieved a worthwhile function.

Preface

'Given: one marketing manager and one accounting manager. Finding: poor communication on financial criteria and goals' (Berry 1977: 125). The risk of this situation's occurring is inevitably present when those with different professional roles are working in accordance with their own norms.

The procedural and legalistic traditions of accounting have not lent themselves to the emerging needs of marketing practitioners, but the onus is primarily on the accountant to relate to the planning, decision-making and control needs of the marketing manager if accounting is to justify its role as a service function in the furtherance of improved organizational effectiveness.

This book seeks to suggest a variety of ways in which accounting systems might be designed and operated to help marketing decision-makers perform more effectively and more efficiently. Whilst the primary market is expected to be made up of aspiring and practising accountants, there is an important secondary market comprising aspiring and practising marketers. Since every holder of a managerial position has responsibility for one or more of resource acquisition, resource allocation and resource utilization, it is necessary that these individuals be *financially literate* given that accounting systems reflect the *lingua franca* of resourcing and – at least to some extent – of performance measurement.

Accountants need to understand the context of marketing if they are to design and operate systems that are useful to marketers, whilst marketers need to be aware of the potential of accounting information to help them in achieving desired marketing outcomes.

Part 1 of the book deals with the setting, and discusses the marketing–accounting interface as well as providing a controllership framework which is reflected in the structure of the book as a whole.

Parts 2 and 3 deal with feedforward and feedback control of marketing activities respectively. There are copious illustrations showing how different approaches might be adopted.

Finally, Part 4 comprises an array of discussion questions, exercises and short cases which provide opportunities for readers to test their grasp of the issues raised.

The author's hope is that this book might make a modest contribution to achieving closer links and greater mutual understanding between accountants and their marketing colleagues in the interests of enhanced organizational effectiveness.

Acknowledgements

Over the long period between the initial commissioning and eventual publication of this book (which included changes of institution on my part as well as a change of publisher) there are various people for whom an acknowledgement is appropriate. I am pleased to record my appreciation to the following:

☐ David Otley, as General Editor of the series, had the vision to include a volume on the theme of *Accounting for Marketing* in the series, and has provided helpful advice on structure and content (but does not deserve the blame for any of the book's shortcomings).

☐ Kim Ansell (at CIMA) and Jennifer Pegg (formerly with Academic Press where the series began but now with ITBP) maintained their faith in the project through some trying times.

☐ Debbie Farr skilfully word-processed the early drafts of the manuscript, and Lynne Atkinson prepared the final version with her characteristic thoroughness and good humour.

☐ My wife, Gillian, maintained a degree of order on the home front which provided me with the space to focus on writing the book.

It is also appropriate to acknowledge the valued influence on my thinking in relation to *Accounting for Marketing* provided by colleagues in the 'college without walls' – especially Ken Simmonds and Stanley Shapiro, to whom this book is dedicated.

With regard to copyright matters, I would like to offer my thanks to the following:

☐ PIMS Associates Ltd (and especially Tony Clayton) for allowing me to base Section 7.3 of Chapter 7 around *The PIMS letter on Business Strategy* Number 47 'How to Think About the Shape of Your Business'.

☐ The Chartered Institute of Marketing for allowing me to include in Part 4 various questions which I compiled whilst with CIM's Senior Examiner responsible for the syllabus of and examinations in *Financial Aspects of Marketing*.

☐ Butterworth-Heinemann for permission to draw on material which is included in Richard M S Wilson and Colin Gilligan, *Strategic Marketing Management: Planning, Implementation and Control*, Second Edition, 1997.

☐ ITPB for permission to draw on material originally included in Richard M S Wilson and Wai Fong Chua, *Managerial Accounting: Method and Meaning*, Second Edition, 1993.

Part 1

The setting

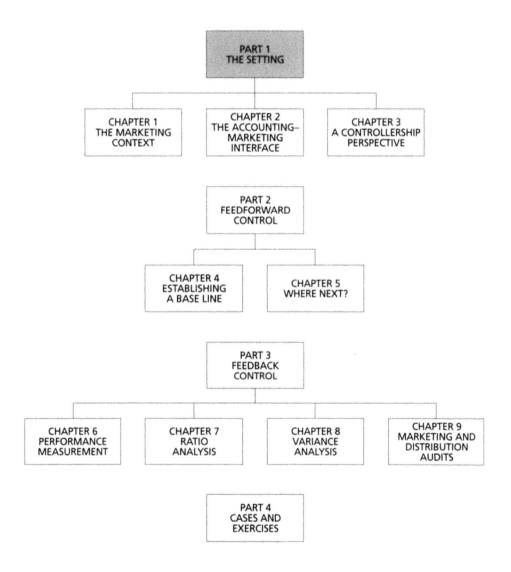

The marketing context $\boxed{1}$

LEARNING OBJECTIVES

After reading this chapter you should be able to:
- ☐ understand the essence of marketing, the marketing concept and marketing orientation;
- ☐ recognize the different eras that preceded the marketing era;
- ☐ appreciate the main financial issues that must be dealt with in a marketing context.

1.1 INTRODUCTION

In considering the philosophies of Britain's leading chief executives, Doyle (1987, 1994) has shown that there has been an excessive emphasis since the late 1970s on developing an increasingly 'right-handed' financially-driven approach (see Figure 1.1). A distinction is made between a concern with the rate of return on investment (ROI) in 'right-handed' companies and a concern with target market share in 'left-handed' companies. An inward focus on cost reduction is typically developed at the expense of focusing outwards on the needs of the marketplace.

From Figure 1.1 it can be seen that the key business decisions relating to product strategy, pricing, distribution and promotion have opposing impacts: there is a left-handed impact on market performance and a right-handed impact on financial results. Britain tends to have lots of right-handed companies whereas Japan has lots of left-handed companies (e.g. Hitachi, Sanyo and Toshiba).

There is a need to balance market and financial requirements. No matter how great his/her abilities may be in other directions, if the marketing manager lacks an understanding of financial concepts he/she will be unable to appreciate fully the end results of his/her planning, and the actions that must be taken to bring these about. In other words, these actions will be beyond his/her control. The financial skill required is largely that of being able to compare the financial outcomes of different courses of action, and appreciating the significance of cost–volume–profit interrelationships.

An enterprise's financial progress is typically measured in terms of profit (preferably related to a capital base), but profits can only arise if the marketing

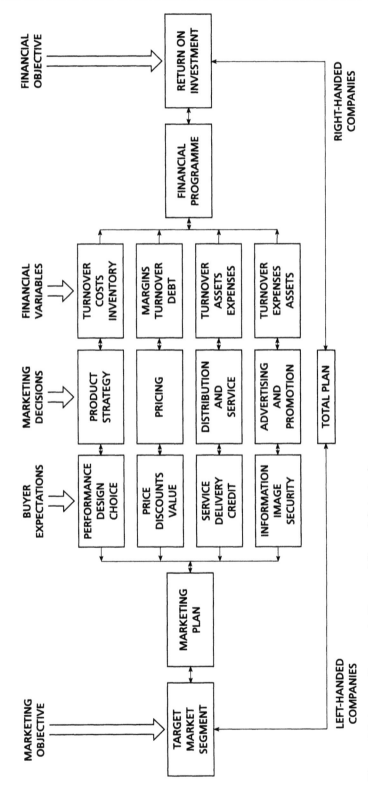

Figure 1.1 Integrating marketing and financial strategies

function is successful in selling that enterprise's goods or services. All the functions of the enterprise incur costs, but only the marketing function generates revenue.

However, marketing management cannot plan its product strategies, means of distribution, pricing policies and other marketing activities in isolation from the other functions of the enterprise. Each marketing manager must be aware of manufacturing costs and their derivation in order to plan his or her own best course of action. But it must not be overlooked that, while an understanding of financial information and techniques is a necessary prerequisite for marketing analysis, this is insufficient in itself. It must be complemented by competent managerial judgement and the ability to influence human behaviour in the desired direction.

Any marketing control system should aim to ensure that sales revenue generated during the period in question is sufficient to achieve the target rate of profit – both physically and economically. This will involve planning to buffer the flow of production with inventory, and will certainly require that a given number of satisfied customers be maintained by the rendering of service factors not directly related to quantities of products, but more concerned with the security of the enterprise (i.e. its continued profitable operation in the long-term future).

The part that the financial controller can play in helping to control the marketing function is only gradually being accepted. The controller has, in fact, been looked upon with either suspicion or doubt as someone who only considered figures whereas marketing executives were convinced that people were more important. At best this made the controller a mere recorder of history – at worst, a positive barrier to progress.

Enlightenment will increase as the profit awareness of marketing management increases further, accompanied by an emphasis on the controller's service function. This service aspect of the controller's work requires that there should be a complete awareness of the enterprise's products, its markets, the marketing organization and the particular problems that marketing management faces. Only armed with this knowledge can the financial controller begin to develop the appropriate control and information systems.

The three major variables with which the marketing manager and the financial controller are concerned are marketing expenditure, market share and profitability. These variables can be displayed graphically to show their interrelationships, as in Figure 1.2.

This graph shows the important point that increasing profit is not necessarily a function of an increasing market share. A frequently met obsession with sales managers is that of maximizing *sales volume*, whereas the action they should be recommending is to optimize *profit*. The relationship between sales and profit should follow one of the following patterns:

1. Increasing sales with a proportionately lower increase in costs improves profit.
2. Increasing sales with constant costs improves profit.
3. Increasing sales and decreasing costs improves profit.
4. Maintaining sales at a constant level but decreasing costs improves profit.
5. Decreasing sales with a proportionately greater decrease in costs improves profit.

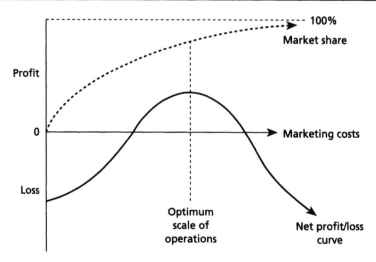

Figure 1.2 Marketing costs, profits and penetration

1.2 THE NATURE OF MARKETING

What is marketing? Many definitions exist with differing emphases on the process of marketing, the functional activities that constitute marketing, and the orientation (or philosophy) of marketing. For example, the Chartered Institute of Marketing defines it as follows:

> Marketing is the management process of identifying, anticipating and satisfying customer requirements profitably.

This 'process' definition can be compared with Drucker's (1973) definition of marketing orientation:

> Marketing is so basic that it cannot be considered a separate function on a par with others such as manufacturing or personnel. It is first a central dimension of the entire business. It is the whole business seen from the point of view of its final result, that is, from the customers' point of view.

A significant shift in emphasis since Drucker wrote this is to be found in the importance that is now attached to competitive position in a changing world. Thus the marketing concept is that managerial orientation which recognizes that success primarily depends upon identifying changing customer wants and developing products and services that match these better than those of competitors (Doyle 1987; see also Wilson and Fook 1990, Wilson and Gilligan 1997, Siu and Wilson 1998).

The contrasting emphases on customers and competitors can be highlighted as in Figure 1.3. If an enterprise is managed a little better than customers expect, and if this is done in a slightly better way than competitors can manage, then the enterprise should be successful.

Within Figure 1.3 the customer-oriented and competitor-centred categories speak for themselves. The self-centred category is characterized by an introspective

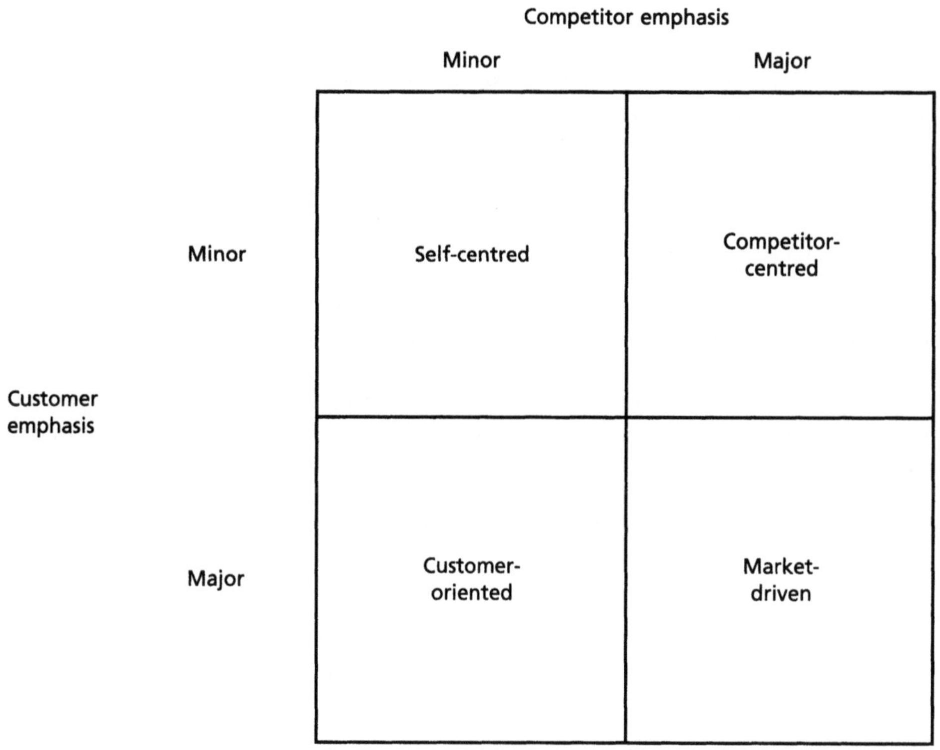

Competitor emphasis

	Minor	Major
Minor	Self-centred	Competitor-centred
Major	Customer-oriented	Market-driven

Customer emphasis

Figure 1.3 Customer and competitor orientations
(Source: adapted from Day 1990: 126)

orientation that focuses on year-on-year improvements in key operating ratios, or on improvements in sales volume without making direct comparisons with competitors. Such an orientation is potentially disastrous when viewed in strategic terms. At the opposite extreme is a market-driven approach to marketing which seeks to balance a responsiveness to customers' requirements on the one hand with direct competitor comparisons on the other.

As pointed out in Wilson (1988: 259), the essential requirements of marketing are:

1. the identification of consumers' needs (covering what goods and services are bought, how they are bought, by whom they are bought, and why they are bought);
2. the definition of target market segments (by which customers are grouped according to common characteristics – demographic, psychological, geographic, etc.);
3. the creation of a differential advantage within target segments by which a distinct competitive position relative to other companies can be established, and from which profit flows.

The way in which a differential advantage might be achieved – and sustained – is via the manipulation of the elements of the *marketing mix*. This mix has traditionally been seen to consist of the 'four Ps' of marketing: product, price, promotion and place. Increasingly, however, but particularly in the service sector, it is being recognized that these four Ps are rather too limited in terms of providing a framework both for thinking about marketing and for planning marketing strategy. It is because of this that a far greater emphasis is now being given to the idea of an expanded mix which has three additional elements (see Figure 1.4):

☐ people
☐ physical evidence
☐ process management.

The increasing acceptance of the marketing concept (whereby the organization looks outwards to the satisfaction of consumers' needs – and those of society – in establishing its competitive position, rather than looking inwards to its entrenched technology) has created a deeper interest in analysing marketing costs for the purposes of establishing marketing strategy and controlling marketing efforts in executing that strategy.

There are two sides to the study of marketing costs. The first of these is concerned with the costs of obtaining orders through such activities as selling, advertising and

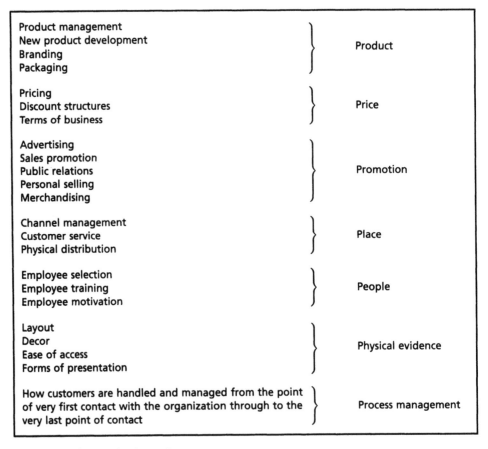

Figure 1.4 The marketing mix

sales promotion. These costs tend to vary with changes in the level of sales, but sales volume will be the dependent variable and order-getting costs will be the independent variable. In other words, sales volume will respond to the level of order-getting costs, and variations in the level of order-getting costs will be made in anticipation of sales being at a predicted level. In this sense, positive management action is needed to permit order-getting costs to increase with increases in sales volume, and, in contrast to manufacturing circumstances, a policy of cost minimization in marketing is unlikely to be desired because of the causal relationship between marketing outlays and sales levels. But the relationship between order-getting costs and sales volume may not be directly linear. For example, a company may increase the amount it is to spend on advertising when sales fall on the basis of the wholly reasonable argument that declining sales require counteractive promotional support to reverse an adverse trend. On the other hand, some companies may maintain the amount to be spent on advertising at some predetermined level (giving it the characteristic of a committed rather than a managed or programmed cost), while still others may unwisely raise advertising expenditure as the level of sales rises and decrease advertising expenditure as sales decline.

The other side of marketing expenditure relates to order-filling activities – warehousing, transportation, shipping, invoicing, credit control, etc. These need to be dealt with in the context of physical distribution management.

Whereas order-filling activities such as warehousing, transportation and materials handling have warranted substantial attention, perhaps because of their more systematic nature, order-getting activities (i.e. the problems of stimulating demand by advertising, selling and pricing in a way that attracts customers) are a relatively deficient area in marketing cost analysis. The following problems arise in dealing with these activities:

1. determining the objectives of advertising, sales promotion, personal selling (and pricing);
2. determining the promotion budget;
3. decisions relating to the allocation of the total marketing effort among varying marketing activities;
4. assessing the effectiveness of marketing effort;
5. identifying profitable/unprofitable marketing segments;
6. decisions relating to where and when a change in marketing effort is required;
7. identifying methods by which segment efficiency may be increased.

A historical perspective

As pointed out by Bancroft and Wilson (1979), Adam Smith neatly summed up a basis from which to begin when he recognized the fact that in the mercantile system the interest of the consumer is almost constantly sacrificed to that of the producer; and it seems to consider production and not consumption as the ultimate end of all industry and commerce.

It is only relatively recently that marketing orientation has been more widely accepted. To understand why this acceptance is so recent and, consequently, the nature of the accounting problems associated with it, it may be helpful to examine the origins of the marketing concept.

It has been possible in reviewing developments over the past hundred years or so to identify three broad eras culminating in what we know today as the *marketing era* (see Harrison 1978). (In considering these eras it must be emphasized that the dates are very approximate and that they correspond roughly to the practices of the more progressive business firms. It should not be assumed that the periods referred to are tightly defined or that the practices of all firms – or even of the average firm – are being described.)

From late in the nineteenth century until about 1930, firms were commonly seen as being established to produce goods with cost accounting developing purely to meet the needs of production management. Even the *Encyclopaedia of Accounting* at the time defined cost accounts thus: 'systematic records of those transactions which relate to manufacturing and are distinct from those accounts dealing with purely commercial, trading or financial affairs. They are closely interwoven with questions of practical factory and workshop administration' (Lisle 1903).

Marketing was not seen as important and any separation of marketing costs from production costs was to enable a better analysis to be made of production itself. It was not thought to be relevant for the cost accountants to concern themselves with costs such as 'discounts on sales interest' and all 'distribution expenses'. These costs were classified on a natural expense basis (e.g. all salaries – as 'natural' expenses – would be aggregated rather than analysed across departments as 'functional' expenses and so forth), which seemed enough to facilitate the book-keeping; and even the phrase 'marketing cost' was little used, 'selling' or 'distribution' expenses being preferred.

This ill-distinction highlighted the lack of understanding of the marketing function on the part of cost accountants. However, from around 1930 there were many new inventions, more consumer-oriented products and a far more competitive environment – bringing out a shift in emphasis to the *sales era*.

The first application of cost accounting to marketing activities became apparent in the post-1930 sales era, although the time devoted to this application was minimal. Nevertheless, there was some realization of the problems involved in determining and controlling marketing costs. Financial analysis for marketing (as for any other function) involves the *functional* classification of marketing costs and their allocation to marketing segments, so determining the costs of the elements within the relevant functions. But the emphasis was on the control of the costs of marketing activities (and the underlying financial analyses) as management was still looking toward profit through *cost control* rather than attempting to identify new profit opportunities (i.e. the emphasis was still on 'after-sale' rather than 'before-sale' activities).

The accountant in this orientation was still dominated by attitudes formed in the production era. A sharp contrast between accountants' introspection (as shown by a frequently encountered preoccupation with the costs of physical activities *within* the company) and the marketing manager's concern with the diagnosis of environmental opportunities (from which the success of an enterprise comes) has been made by a number of writers, such as Simmonds (1970), Williamson (1979) and Wilson (1975, 1979, 1981).

Various studies have highlighted the fact that there appeared to be a misdirection of marketing effort, due mainly to a lack of knowledge of the interaction of the firm's products and markets. However, the nature of the business, the markets, the customers and channels of distribution were being investigated for the first time during the sales

	Focus	Means	End
Sales concept	Products	Selling and promoting	Profits through sales volume and cost control
Marketing concept	Customers' needs	Integrated marketing	Profits through customer satisfaction

Figure 1.5 Sales and marketing orientations compared

era, although the time devoted to marketing planning and control was seemingly negligible compared with that spent on production management.

The change from the sales era has brought us into the period denoted as the *marketing era*, reflecting the emergence and adoption of the *marketing concept*, apparent from 1950. Kotler (1967) defined this as 'a customer orientation backed by integrated marketing aimed at generating customer satisfaction as a key to satisfying organizational goals'. Marketing was thereby placed at the beginning of the business process, determining which products were needed, at what prices and how they were to be promoted and distributed. Figure 1.5 shows how it contrasts with the sales concept.

There was an increased emphasis on reporting and on the analysis of information to aid marketing management in planning and control. The opportunity had arisen for the closer involvement of the accountant in helping solve problems in the marketing function.

1.3 SUMMARY

Within this chapter we have considered the nature of marketing and some of the characteristics of marketing orientation. A clear distinction was drawn between the introspective orientation with its focus on cost reduction (which is characteristic of accountants and 'right-handed' companies) and the outward-looking orientation of 'left-handed' companies (which reflects the adoption of a marketing approach).

We saw that the key elements within marketing can be classified as either *order-getting* or *order-filling* activities, and together these make up the marketing mix.

For a marketing manager to be effective it is necessary, *inter alia*, for him or her to be financially aware and to recognize, for example, that maximizing sales volume is not necessarily helpful in seeking to optimize profit outcomes.

2 The accounting– marketing interface

LEARNING OBJECTIVES

After reading this chapter you should be able to:
- ☐ recognize the need for effective communication and mutual understanding between marketers and accountants if marketing control is to be achieved;
- ☐ appreciate the differences between the control of manufacturing operations and the control of marketing activities, and how to overcome problems relating to the latter;
- ☐ understand different definitions of cost in a way that avoids an introspective fixation on manufacturing activities.

2.1 INTRODUCTION

If business enterprise succeeds through the creation of utilities, it seems rather anomalous that the background of the typical management accountant reflects an introspective fixation with production (and the utility of form) rather than a broader concern with marketing (and the creation of the utilities of time, place and ownership).

Given that we are effective to the extent that we achieve that which we set out to achieve, and that we are efficient if we use minimum input to achieve a given output (or achieve maximum output for a given input), it can be suggested that measuring and improving the profitability and efficiency of marketing operations is an important element in increasing organizational effectiveness.

Measuring and improving the profitability and efficiency of marketing operations requires knowledge of the costs and revenues associated with marketing activities, which can be viewed from at least two directions:

1. the analysis of costs, revenues and profits of past marketing activities – the *ex post* approach that is characteristic of an accounting orientation;
2. the assessment of the financial implications of proposed courses of marketing action (involving the prospective allocation of resources to opportunities that have been identified in the organization's environment) – the *ex ante* approach that is characteristic of marketing orientation.

Rather than adopting one of these approaches to the exclusion of the other, it is essential to accounting–marketing integration to consider them together and to relate them to a common set of problems. These problems are the nature and magnitude of marketing costs; the interaction of volume, costs and profits; and the productivity of marketing actions.

By considering the problems of cost definitions and levels, the interrelationships of cost, volume and revenue, and the productivity of marketing outlays, we have a base from which to promote better decision-making, which is a prime determinant of organizational effectiveness. But this takes us into the consideration of a sequence of related matters.

Better decisions depend, *inter alia*, on better definitions of problems requiring solutions and on the generation of better potential solutions from which a choice (i.e. decision) must be made. Both these matters (problem definition and potential solutions) depend upon the availability of better information, which – at least in part – depends upon the techniques available (i.e. the state of accounting technology in this context) for supplying information.

At this point, it is as well to consider the 'specialised ears and generalised deafness' that Boulding (1956) stated to be so characteristic of the specialist world of the advanced economies. If accounting systems are to be designed to reflect the decision-making needs of marketing users, this suggests that accountants should seek an understanding of the problems and operating conditions facing marketing managers. Equally, of course, there is some onus on marketing managers to get behind the mystique that tends to surround accounting methods, statements and terminology, and demand a comprehensible and useful service from their organizations' accounting functions rather than having to tolerate something 'designed' many years ago to suit accountants' convenience in discharging their stewardship role.

These issues are incorporated in Figure 2.1 which (working from the left-hand side) suggests that functional specialists – whether in marketing or management accounting – will improve communications if they take active steps to learn about their counterparts' functions. Improved understanding coupled with more relevant information should lead to better marketing decisions. This in turn should lead to improved organizational effectiveness.

2.2 A COMPARISON OF MANAGEMENT ACCOUNTING FOR MANUFACTURING AND MARKETING

In many companies, the costs of marketing greatly exceed manufacturing costs, yet relatively little attention has been given to the analysis of marketing costs compared to the extensive attention given to manufacturing costs. It is instructive to consider some of the reasons for this state of affairs, and these include the following:

1. While the costs of productive labour and materials can be associated with specific machines, processes and products, the costs of the elements of the marketing mix cannot be associated so readily with outputs (such as sales and profit levels).
2. Marketing activities tend to be less routine and repetitive than is the case with many standardized production activities.

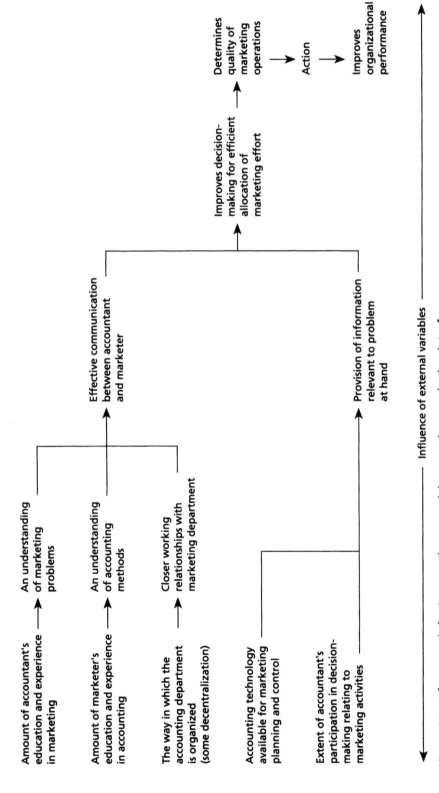

Figure 2.1 A framework for improved managerial accounting–marketing interface
(Source: Bancroft and Wilson 1979: 29)

3. The dependency of marketing activities on outside agencies distinguishes them further from the more internally-regulated and predictable manufacturing activities.

4. Marketing activities tend to be performed in many locations – often distant from each other – rather than on one site.

5. Within manufacturing there is the relatively simple choice to be made between using the product or using the process as the cost object. In contrast, within marketing there are many more possible cost objects – such as the product line, product range, customer, customer/industry group, sales person, sales territory, size of order and channel of distribution.

6. The cost behaviour patterns of many marketing activities are the reverse of those for manufacturing activities in the sense that (order-getting) marketing costs tend to determine sales volume (hence manufacturing costs). Order-getting costs are committed in anticipation of sales. Whereas manufacturing costs necessarily increase as sales volume rises, order-getting costs must be permitted to increase. Thus, for a given level of activity, the lower the manufacturing costs the better, while the right level (and mix) of order-getting costs is a matter of judgement. It can be argued that the 'best' approach is to focus on technical efficiency in relation to order-getting outlays (i.e. to maximize the outputs for a given level of input), and on economic efficiency in relation to manufacturing and order-filling outlays (whereby one aims to minimize the inputs for a given level of output). This indicates the analytical complexity inherent in accounting for marketing costs – whether order-getting or order-filling.

7. Since marketing costs are rarely included in inventory valuations (being treated instead as period costs) financial accounting principles, etc., provide little incentive for detailed analysis.

8. Manufacturing activities typically have a short-run focus whereas marketing operations must pay attention to long-run considerations. This also produces a conflict over financial accounting practice in that promotional outlays in a particular period are invariably matched with the sales achieved during that period notwithstanding the fact that much promotional expenditure (and other order-getting outlays) are in the nature of capital investment intended to stimulate sales over several time periods.

9. Personnel in manufacturing roles often have a greater cost-consciousness and discipline than their marketing colleagues.

10. The risk of sub-optimization (whereby one particular aspect is maximized to the possible detriment of the whole) is much greater in a complex marketing context than it is in manufacturing.

11. Many marketing activities have an intangible quality that distinguishes them from the tangible characteristics of production activities. Among the intangible factors is the psychological dimension of purchase predisposition.

2.3 PROBLEMS IN MANAGEMENT ACCOUNTING FOR MARKETING

It is invariably found that the costs stemming from marketing activities are difficult to plan and control. The lowest costs are not necessarily to be preferred, since these may not result in the effective attainment of the desired sales volume and profit. Most order-getting costs are programmed rather than variable, and tend to influence the volume of sales rather than be influenced by it.

The characteristics of marketing costs lead to problems in analysis. Such characteristics include:

1. Long-run effects (e.g. the effect of an advertising campaign lasts longer than the campaign, and is usually lagged).
2. The difficulty in measuring productivity, since standards are not easily determined. (Standards can be set for sales activities – e.g. cost to create £1 of sales revenue, average cost of each unit sold, cost to generate £1 of profit, cost per transaction, cost per customer serviced. However, in product decisions, levels of performance may be expressed in terms of the minimum required level of sales/revenue per product line, or the minimum profit contribution required.)
3. The non-symmetrical nature of costs. (For example, costs increase more in changing from regional to national distribution than would be saved by changing from national to regional distribution.)
4. Costs are frequently indivisible or joint costs, often intended to support a product group.
5. Some costs have discontinuities or a stepped-character shape.

Planning in the light of these characteristics must be based to a significant extent on past experience, knowledge of competitive activities, test marketing exercises, and the estimated expenditure that desired profits at various levels of activity will permit.

Accounting data in the more conventional form provides a point of departure for marketing cost analyses, but these data must be re-worked on the basis of units that are subject to management control. (The relevant control unit will depend on the purpose of the analysis, but may be a product, product line, sales territory, marketing division, customer group, etc.)

But the difficulties of developing and successfully applying management accounting techniques in marketing are compounded by a multitude of further factors that are not primarily financial, among which are the following:

6. Plans must be based on sales forecasts. If the forecast of projected sales exceeds the firm's productive capacity, the firm may be required to expand its production facilities, raise prices (to ration available output) or subcontract, only to find that the forecast was too high. Conversely, the forecast may predict insufficient sales to produce the desired ROI. In this event, the firm may alter its sales coverage, extend credit carelessly, introduce inadequately tested new products, and so forth, in an attempt to increase the sales volume. Should the original forecast have been low, the actions taken subsequently may be against the firm's better interests.
7. The outputs of the marketing sub-system intimately affect the outputs of the firm's other sub-systems. In turn, the next outputs of these other sub-systems will affect the further outputs of the marketing sub-system. The solution can only come from a greater intra-organizational understanding of what is in the interests of the firm as a whole.
8. The enormous range of strategic possibilities makes it impossible to include all of them in a formal analysis. Any particular marketing strategy will involve a particular combination of the elements of the marketing mix, with particular

Figure 2.2 The influence of external factors
(Source: Wilson 1983: 209)

assumed environmental conditions. The number of different possible combinations is vast. This does not mean that quantitative techniques are useless, but it does mean that measurement problems arise to complicate the issue (see Gilligan and Wilson 2000).

9. The ever-changing environment – including the impacts of competitive activities, developments in technology, changes in consumer tastes, government action, and the other factors depicted in Figure 2.2 – makes planning difficult. As a result, control is made more difficult since it is no longer clear which variances were avoidable and which unavoidable.

10. In considering the range of possible strategies, the uncertainty that any one constituent factor may change at almost any time makes the question of choice even more difficult.

11. The effectiveness of costs (i.e. productivity or efficiency) is not easy to measure. The interdependent variety of elements involved and their varying long- and short-run effects are the cause of this difficulty. For example, the respective contributions of advertising and direct selling activities to the sales level are not readily separable.

12. The tendency towards globalization, with its attendant diversification of activities and sheer size, results in an increasing complexity that challenges the best efforts in securing control.

13. The interface of the marketing sub-system with external agencies is fraught with difficulties. The firm's control over the performance of these agencies (such as wholesalers, shippers and advertising agents) depends upon the degree of independence of each, and the nature of the relationship.

14. The human element (in the form of sales staff, product managers and other marketing personnel, added to the all-important consumer) creates further problems. Marketing is centred upon this human factor, while production is centred upon more inanimate factors.

15. Finally, problems arise in connection with special marketing projects, such as the development of a new product, a major advertising campaign or entry into a new territory. The problem is the usual one of correctly evaluating the profit and cost aspects of the project, and then keeping within budgeted expense limits and time schedules.

Although these problems are many, they do not mean that no attempts should be made to successfully plan and control marketing activities. However, there is evidence to show that most accountants are not yet in tune with marketing thinking. First, accountants lack the knowledge and understanding of the information requirements necessary for the marketing function. Second, accountants do not accept marketing as a distinct and separate managerial function. This seemingly blind attitude was found in a survey (reported by Williamson 1979) to be well ingrained and is an appalling indication of the failure of accountants to see the real essence of business activity (i.e. product–market interactions) and of a misplaced arrogance in looking down on a group whose purpose and function they so clearly misunderstand. Lastly, organizational design may impede adequate communications between functions. This could (and does) happen to such an extent that the accounting and marketing departments may be geographically diverse from one another, although marketing activities are geographically diverse in any event.

A long-established organizational design could also hinder a new pattern of resource allocation. It may be such that available resources are channelled towards the order-filling production and distribution functions rather than to the order-getting processes such as advertising, sales promotion and selling. Allocating to the former in preference to the latter is tantamount to saying that a firm can sell what it can make – the old sales concept – rather than the marketing concept of making what consumers want.

The practical consequences of these inhibitions manifest themselves in the following ways:

Schiff and Mellman (1962), in a pioneering US empirical study, noted deficiencies of the accounting function in supplying marketing with sufficient information in certain areas, such as:

1. lack of effective financial analyses of customers, channels of distribution and sales staff;
2. an over-emphasis on net-profit-based reporting (or the full-cost allocation approach);
3. inadequacies in marketing cost classification (e.g. little distinction was made between fixed and variable costs or between controllable and non-controllable costs);
4. return on investment was rarely used; and
5. there was a general lack of integration between the accounting and marketing functions.

Goodman (1970a), in a later US study, found that accounting did not appear to have made much progress in satisfying the needs of marketing planning. These areas of failure he saw as being:

1. non-use of sufficient return-on-investment criteria;
2. insistence on using the traditional full-costing for decision analyses;
3. inability to separate the reporting obligation of accounting from the service function;
4. imperfect understanding of the marketing concept;
5. lack of minimum acceptable goal criteria; and
6. disregard for the implications of working capital.

As various authorities have observed, there are fundamental differences between accounting and marketing. For example, accounting builds from an analysis of internal financial data whereas marketing builds from the diagnosis of external market situations. The respective perspectives are literally poles apart (see Simmonds 1981b). Thus the marketing view that profit stems from a firm's position relative to its competitors (i.e. reflecting its differential advantage) and is not a function of arbitrary financial periods is not likely to meet with full-blooded approval – or even understanding – on the part of the average accountant who invariably fails to link his or her own measures to either market share or changes in market size. Among the explanations for this difference in perspectives is the idea of there being a 'cultural lag' between the two disciplines (i.e. accounting and marketing). There are many definitions of 'culture' but, broadly speaking, it refers to the learned patterns of behaviour and symbolism which are passed from generation to generation and which represent the total of values that characterize society (and the behaviour of individuals within it). One can also characterize the behaviour of members of different professional groupings in accordance with cultural criteria. The values etc. that accountants espouse as a consequence of their training – which is a process of socialization and, in a sense, indoctrination – are the cultural signs of accountants that distinguish them from, say, marketing specialists, who espouse different values.

Field and Gabhart (1971) identified a cultural lag between accounting and other disciplines in that there appears to be a resistance (on the part of accounting) to change and a failure to take a more sophisticated view, especially in costing and valuation.

Briefly, cultural lag occurs when one element of culture changes more rapidly than another. In business and professional fields this occurs when knowledge developed in one field takes several years to filter down to affect practice. Alternatively, knowledge that is available in a particular field may not be applied to or integrated with functionally-related theory and practice in a neighbouring discipline where some elements are interdependent. The latter has occurred in the case of accounting.

At first sight accounting and marketing may appear completely distinct but perhaps, on close scrutiny, they are inseparable. For example, Simmonds (1970) sees marketing as a part of management thinking concerned with making decisions against a marketplace. Management accounting is also fundamental to management decisions in providing some of the necessary information. Simmonds holds that both fields are defined and therefore justified by their contribution to the management task. The management objective at any particular time determines the contribution that is needed from each. Given this argument, however, he feels that a general business training is needed and that the professions of accounting and marketing cannot, in the interests of organizations, be kept apart, because then they would become less relevant. He sees the need for accountants to join with other professions for sounder decision-making.

For efficient marketing there is a need for salient data and, as much of this is only available from accounting, Field and Gabhart understandably express concern about their being 'as non-integrated as cats and dogs'.

2.4 THE NATURE OF COST

In Chapter 3 we consider how to locate managerial accounting within an organizational control context. Managerial accounting does not exist for its own sake: it exists to enable managers to make better decisions and thereby improve the effectiveness of their organizations.

We can think of organizations – whether commercial or non-commercial, manufacturing or service-rendering, large or small – as consisting of a cluster of projects or activities. Take a college or university as an example: it is made up of degree programmes, recreational activities, committees carrying out assigned briefs, and so on. This mix of projects and activities is ever-changing – thus a new degree scheme combining accounting and organizational analysis might be added, and the students' union's involvement in anti-nuclear activities might be terminated. Every project has resource implications, and the shortage of resources invariably means that choices must be made in rationing available resources among competing projects. It may be the case that new projects can only be taken on by an enterprise if old ones are dropped, thereby freeing some resources.

In establishing a base line for assessing the effectiveness with which an enterprise is carrying out its various activities it is helpful to know the cost of those activities. Since we use the term 'cost' in everyday parlance we probably take its meaning for granted. However, in dealing with the resource implications of existing (or prospective) projects and activities we need to consider carefully the nature of 'cost' in its many forms. Everything that a manager does, as well as many things he or she fails to do, has an associated cost. This is not to suggest that the costs of taking (or not taking) a particular course of action are all identifiable or measurable. But it does beg the question of what is meant by 'cost'. (The emphasis given here to *cost* does not mean that revenue, profit and profitability are unimportant. It simply reflects the greater difficulty that is typically experienced in defining and measuring marketing costs in an appropriate way.)

Cost defined

In accounting, costs are usually defined as those outlays (or expenses) that cause a reduction in assets – such as the payment of rents and wages – with cash (a current asset) being reduced as payments are made.

Anthony and Reece (1983) define cost in accounting terms as follows: 'Cost is a measurement, in monetary terms, of the amount of resources used for some purpose' (p. 549). Particular points to highlight within this definition are:

☐ it requires *monetary* measurement;
☐ it involves *resources*;
☐ it needs a *purpose* to be specified.

It helps in clarifying terminological difficulties within accounting to introduce a time dimension. Cost in accounting is the amount of resource that is given up (or exchanged) at a point in time for a particular purpose, as measured in monetary terms, e.g. the price paid on 30 November to acquire a word processor. (In this sense, cost is a *valuation* concept: under the historic cost convention the value of the word processor can be expressed in terms of the cost of acquiring ownership of it.) At the time the word processor is purchased it has service potential over its future life, and hence is classified as an asset (thereby ensuring inclusion in the enterprise's balance sheet). As the service potential is consumed this is shown as an expense in the profit and loss account of each period benefiting from the asset's services. In the case of the word processor (as with other fixed assets) this diminution of service potential is represented by the depreciation charges in successive profit and loss accounts.

For financial reporting purposes this may be satisfactory, but for decision-making (and hence control) purposes it is necessary to define cost in a way that reflects economic reality a little better. Costs are defined by economists in terms of forgone alternatives (or opportunities). Thus the cost of a given input into a system is the maximum value that the input in question could generate in an alternative use. If its use precludes its sale, for example, then its cost is its net realizable value (i.e. what it could have been sold for, less the costs of selling it).

Cost is characterized by the word *sacrifice* and, as such, it is very much in management's interests to control and reduce where possible the sacrifices involved in achieving desired results. In this broad sense cost is equivalent to sacrifices of various types, although they are not all reflected in a company's cash flow.

Different costs for different purposes

It is important to recognize that the term 'cost' only has meaning in a given context and always requires an adjective accompanying it to avoid confusion. There are different cost concepts that are appropriate for different purposes, and no single cost concept is relevant to all situations.

The expression 'different costs for different purposes' has been widely used, and can be traced back to the title of Chapter 9 of J.M. Clark's classic book, *Studies in the Economics of Overhead Costs* (1923: 175). Clark presented nine different decisions and showed how each needed different cost data. Since then the expression has been rather abused and is often taken to mean that users might need different measures of the cost of a given thing. This is not likely since (as mentioned in the previous paragraph) 'cost' requires an adjective (e.g. full, direct) before it can be operationalized, and the cost object of interest also needs to be defined. Thus we might wish to know the *full* cost of carrying out a particular research study, or the *direct* cost of using local carriers as opposed to operating our own delivery vehicles.

To be sure, we need to associate appropriate concepts of cost with the *cost objects* that concern us, and the specification of the purpose to be served will eliminate any major ambiguity. We may want to know how much effort (in the form of resources) is being allocated to the manufacture of product X, and a measure of the full product cost of X will give us this information. However, once we know this it may prompt the question: 'Should we continue manufacturing product X?' In order to answer this we would have to seek a more appropriate measure of cost than full cost. This would be given by the *avoidable* costs (rather than the *full* cost) associated with manufacturing X.

Any controversy should disappear once it is recognized that 'there are different kinds of problems for which we need information about costs, and the particular information we need differs from one problem to another' (Clark 1923: 35).

If we take an example concerning the *full* cost of a compact disc player this may be (from your point of view) £150 that you would have to pay to buy one (plus, perhaps, the cost of any hi-fi guide you bought to help you choose the best model for your purpose, the cost of a plug and the transport costs you incur in acquiring the CD player). But, from the point of view of either the dealer who sold the CD player to you or the organization that manufactured it, determining its full cost is much more problematic!

The clarification of cost categories

Many of the costs of marketing are not satisfactorily identified since marketing functions are not always carried out by the marketing department. (It could be argued that any members of an organization who deal with customers, for example, are carrying out a marketing function even though they may not be recognized in any formal sense as members of the marketing staff.) This is one definitional problem, but not the only one.

In their training, management accountants are almost indoctrinated to think, for example, of variable costs as being manufacturing costs that fluctuate with the level of production output, or to define direct costs as those that can be readily traced to units of manufactured output, and so on. It is imperative that a broader view be taken in order that the analysis of marketing costs might be tackled.

In this general sense we can define costs in the following ways:

1. A fixed cost is one that does not vary in relation to changes in the level of activity (however defined) within a given period of time.
2. A variable cost is one that varies in proportion to changes in the level of activity (however defined).

This distinction facilitates flexible budgeting, permits cost–volume–profit analysis, and gives a basis for flexible pricing. However, the further distinction between avoidable and unavoidable costs needs to be considered since it cannot safely be assumed that a fixed cost is inevitably unavoidable. Much will depend on whether a particular fixed cost is 'committed', 'managed' or 'discretionary': this last could almost certainly be avoided in the short term if a better use for the resources in question were available, although a committed fixed cost would not be easily avoided other than in the long run.

The base (i.e. level of activity) to be used in determining cost behaviour patterns must be carefully selected and have a clear causal relationship with the level of cost in question. In this regard it must not be assumed that sales volume causes order-getting costs. Let us consider some examples:

(a) Advertising and sales promotion costs are not caused by sales volume since sales volume is the dependent (rather than the independent) variable. The advertising budget is likely to be a fixed sum per period of time representing a programmed, managed or discretionary cost.
(b) Personal selling costs are rather more complicated: commissions will tend to vary with sales volume (or value); salaries will be a fixed cost of a managed

type that is independent of sales volume within any given financial period; and expenses will be a mixture of fixed and variable costs that are also independent of sales volume. Suitable bases for determining cost behaviour patterns may be number of calls made, number of customers, distance travelled, etc.

3. A direct cost is one that can be specifically traced to a cost object. In a marketing context, as mentioned earlier, this object may be any one of several alternatives other than the product. Thus, in an analysis of sales territories, the salaries, commissions and expenses of sales personnel working exclusively in one territory constitute direct costs of that territory.

4. An indirect cost is one that cannot be traced to a specific cost object on anything other than a largely arbitrary basis. The more specific a cost object is (e.g. a customer or a product line), the greater will be the proportion of costs that are indirect, whereas the more broadly based is a cost object (e.g. a sales territory), the greater will be the proportion of costs that can be traced directly to it. It should be borne in mind, however, that direct costs can be fixed or variable in nature (and similarly with indirect costs), so directness should not be linked in any general way with variable costs alone – whether in a marketing or in any other setting.

5. A controllable cost is one that can be influenced by an individual whose performance is being measured by reference to such costs. Thus a sales manager will be held accountable for his or her sales team's expenses on the grounds that he or she can influence – and hence control – their rate of incurrence. Controllable costs, then, usually originate in the sphere of organizational responsibility under consideration.

6. An uncontrollable cost is one that cannot be influenced by a particular individual (e.g. a manager cannot specify his/her own salary, so this is an uncontrollable cost from the viewpoint of his/her level of authority). It would, in general terms, be unreasonable to judge an individual's performance by reference to significant amounts of uncontrollable costs.

   Controllable costs will often – but not always – be variable in nature. However, it is unusual for any fixed costs to be controllable in the short run unless they are clearly discretionary or programmed (which will frequently include some order-getting costs, such as advertising appropriations that have not yet been irrevocably committed).

   It is not usually considered reasonable to hold an individual accountable for apportioned costs – such as may relate to head-office services to divisions. Nevertheless, if one is interested in the performance of the division (rather than its manager) it may be appropriate to make cautious allocations of uncontrollable costs. (This is the basis of productivity analysis which will be discussed in Chapter 4 starting on p. 46.)

7. A standard cost is one that represents the efficient performance of a repetitive task. This will include the direct labour and material inputs in a manufacturing situation, but it is by no means limited to the production arena. Distribution activities as well as certain clerical tasks are amenable to cost standards, and a range of marketing cost standards can also be developed. (This topic will be covered in Chapter 5 – see the section starting on p. 72.)

Yet another definitional problem concerns the focus that management accountants should adopt in seeking to render a service to their marketing colleagues. If the management accountant perceives his or her terms of reference as stemming from the traditional accounting preoccupation with product costing, thereby emphasizing the attributes of what is currently being made, he or she will fail to offer analyses that emphasize patterns of consumer preferences and competitive positioning by market segment. The attributes of market segments – from which profit derives – are fundamentally different from those attributes that characterize the production process. Any analysis that is based on product cost will inevitably generate insights that are limited by their origins, thereby failing to support marketing orientation.

The usual approach of accountants has been termed 'data-oriented': the recording, analysing and reporting of data is determined by what is available. Such an approach neither answers nor asks the critical questions concerning the problems of the marketplace that require diagnosing and solving. The remedy is to redefine the management accountant's role in terms of an 'information orientation' by which marketing problems are examined to determine information needs from which the required information can then be generated to assist marketing managers.

2.5 SUMMARY

Within this chapter we have been concerned with the *interface* between marketing and management accounting in order to see the need for improved communications and greater mutual understanding if marketing control is to be effective. The risk of 'specialized ears and generalized deafness' is always present, given the emphasis on manufacturing that is characteristic of accountants' training and the aversion to financial matters that is widespread among both established and aspiring marketers.

Many reasons can be put forward to show why the control of marketing activities is problematic and how it differs from the control of manufacturing operations. Complexity, predictive limitations and the human element are primary factors, along with a cultural lag.

In conceiving of any organization as a bundle of projects it becomes necessary to define the projects (e.g. as missions, activities, segments) and to identify the costs, revenues and associated assets in order to determine their productivity and profitability. One inhibiting factor is the tendency for accountants to think of costs in an inappropriate way due to their introspective emphasis on manufacturing processes and products.

Within a marketing context there are many different cost objects and clear definitions of cost categories are needed to ensure that useful information is provided to marketing decision-makers.

A controllership perspective

3

LEARNING OBJECTIVES

After reading this chapter you should be able to:
- ☐ recognize the need for control to be exercised in the context of marketing activities;
- ☐ appreciate the key features of control and the essential steps involved in designing control systems;
- ☐ distinguish between *control* and *controls*;
- ☐ understand the role of the marketing controller.

3.1 INTRODUCTION TO CONTROL

Since control is a process whereby management ensures that the organization is achieving desired ends, it can be defined as a set of organized (adaptive) actions directed towards achieving a specified goal in the face of constraints.

To bring about particular future events it is necessary to influence the factors that lie behind those events. It is the ability to bring about a desired future outcome at will that is the essence of control. In this sense it can be seen that control itself is a *process* and not an event. Moreover, the idea of control can be seen to be synonymous with such notions as adaptation, influence, manipulation and regulation. But control in the sense in which the term is used in this book is *not* synonymous with coercion. Nor does it have as its central feature (as so often seems to be thought) the detailed study of past mistakes, but rather the focusing of attention on current and, more particularly, on future activities to ensure that they are carried through in a way that leads to desired ends.

The existence of a control process enables management to know from time to time where the organization stands in relation to a predetermined future position. This requires that progress can be observed, measured and re-directed if there are discrepancies between the actual and the desired positions.

Control and planning are complementary, so each should logically presuppose the existence of the other. Planning presupposes objectives (ends), and objectives are of very limited value in the absence of a facilitating plan (means) for their attainment. In the planning process management must determine the organization's

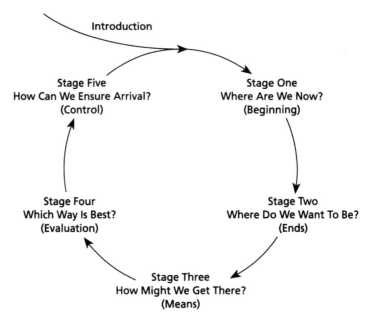

Figure 3.1 A framework for marketing planning and control
(Source: Wilson and Gilligan 1997: 6)

future course of action by reconciling corporate resources with specified corporate objectives. This will usually involve a consideration of various alternative courses of action and the selection of the one that is seen to be the best in the light of the objectives. Figure 3.1 shows a framework for marketing planning and control that explicitly identifies the need for evaluation in choosing between alternative means.

In seeking to exercise control it is important to recognize that the process is inevitably value-laden: the preferred future state that one is seeking to realize is unlikely to be the same for individual A as for individual B, and that which applies to individuals also, within limits, applies to organizations. Only human actors can decide what future outcomes they want to bring about, and in specifying these they set goals for oganizations.

In seeking to exercise control the major hindrances are uncertainty (since the relevant time horizon for control is the future, which cannot be totally known in advance) and the inherent complexity of socio-economic and socio-technical systems (such as business organizations). If one had an adequate understanding of the ways in which complex organizations function, and if this facilitated reliable predictions, then the information stemming from this predictive understanding would enable one to control the organization's behaviour. In this sense it can be seen that information and control have an equivalence.

Behind the presumption, therefore, that we can control anything there is an implied assertion that we know enough about the situation in question (e.g. what is being sought, how well things are going, what is going wrong, how matters might be put right). But do we actually know these things?

The concept of organizational control

The word 'control' is widely used in everyday talk and in scientific language. Herein lies the difficulty. Because it is widely used it means different things to different people in different settings. Indeed, Rathe (1960) showed that there were some '57 varieties' (borrowing the term from Mr Heinz) of the word. The most common meaning is that of dominance, as in A has control over B. But this represents only one possible meaning of the term.

In order to carefully define what we mean by organizational control we shall draw on cybernetics. This has been defined by one of its founders, Wiener (1948), as 'the science of control and communication in the animal and the machine'. This definition suggests the disciplines in which cybernetics has had the most impact – physics, biology and engineering. However, as a theory of control, cybernetics is sufficiently general to be of interest to those who are interested in managing human organizations.

In cybernetics, control has two distinctive aspects:

☐ Control is related to the regulation and monitoring of activities.
☐ Control involves the taking of actions that will ensure that desired ends are attained. Control is therefore related to some notion of goals and of purpose.

We may compare this cybernetic definition of control with an ordinary, everyday use of the term. Ordinary language use connotes the word 'control' in two main ways:

1. A situation that is 'in control' is seen generally as 'a good thing'. A situation that is 'out of control' is usually considered bad or undesirable. Think of a car, an epidemic, a school class or an economy that is out of control. These situations all carry negative connotations.
2. To be in control implies a prior notion of proper, desired behaviour. For example, a car or a class of students cannot be said to be 'out of control' unless we have a preconceived idea of how a car ought to function and a class to behave. Therefore, we need a statement of 'what ought to happen', or desired behaviour, in order to know whether uncontrollable behaviour exists.

From an analysis of cybernetic and everyday usage of the term, we note that control:

☐ is related to the regulation and monitoring of activities;
☐ involves the taking of actions that ensure that desired ends are met.

Organizational control may be defined to take account of these important aspects of control. Following Otley and Berry (1980: 233), we shall define organizational control as:

> The process of ensuring that the organization is pursuing courses of action that will enable it to achieve its purposes.

3.2 BASIC CONTROL CONCEPTS

In this section (which draws on Wilson and Chua 1993), we will distinguish between:

☐ open-loop control; and
☐ closed-loop control.

We shall also distinguish between two main forms of closed-loop control:

☐ feedforward control; and
☐ feedback control.

To some extent, therefore, the following discussion will act as a preface to Part 2 of the book insofar as it deals with feedforward control, and as a preface to Part 3 insofar as it deals with feedback control.

(a) Open-loop control

This form of control exists when an attempt is made by a system (for example, an organization) to achieve some desired goal, but no adjustments are made to its actions once the sequence of intended acts is under way. A very simple example is that of a golfer hitting a golf ball: his/her aim is to get the ball into the hole, and with this in mind he/she will take into account the distance, the hazards, and so forth, prior to hitting the ball. Once the ball is in the air there is nothing that the golfer can do but hope that he/she did things right.

To take another example, suppose a company wished to sell 100 000 micro-computers over the next 12 months. Its managers would gear the company up to promote, manufacture and distribute the product at a predetermined price in the light of various assumptions regarding likely patterns of demand, possible competitive actions, and so on. If the company blindly proceeded to carry out its marketing, manufacturing and distribution plans without any modifications to take into account changes in its environment (e.g. competitive reactions in the form of price reductions) this would be an example of open-loop control. Within such a system there is a goal, a plan, but no mechanism to ensure that the plan is accomplished.

Two possible refinements to the basic open-loop model are:

(i) To introduce a monitoring device for the continual scanning of both the environment and the transformation process of the system (that is, the process by which the organization converts inputs into outputs). This will provide a basis for modifying either initial plans or the transformation process itself if it appears that circumstances are likely to change before the plan has run its course and the goal has been realized. This is *feedforward control*, and is illustrated in Figure 3.2.

Some examples of feedforward systems might be useful, and the following are commonly found:

☐ *Cash planning*, whereby an organization's cash balance is maintained at some desired level.

☐ *Inventory control*, whereby the balance of each item of inventory is regulated at a desired level. The process comprises the procurement, storing and issuing of raw materials, components, finished goods and other supplies. Inventory records contain the necessary measurements, and the regulator may be either a member of the stores personnel or a computer.

The key input variable to an inventory feedforward control system will be either the anticipated level of sales of finished goods (in a marketing operation)

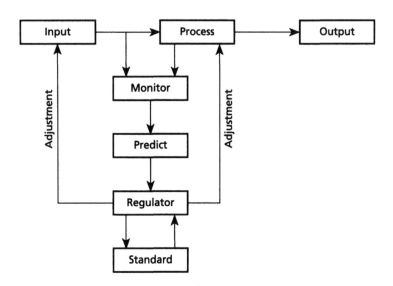

Figure 3.2 A feedforward control system

or the rate of usage of materials/supplies (in a manufacturing or service operation). Other input variables will include:
- amount of purchases
- returns (whether of sales or purchases)
- spoilage
- shrinkage
- lead times (between ordering goods and receiving deliveries).

While it can be argued that the characteristic to be controlled is the balance of each item held in inventory, it will be apparent that this is a function of stock-holding costs and the target level of service to be offered.

☐ *New product development* (NPD), which aims to introduce successful new products with an efficient use of resources. This requires careful coordination between the R & D, marketing research, engineering, manufacturing, marketing, distribution and finance functions. Feedforward control can help by regulating the timing of related activities and the quality of results.

NPD is a good example of a *project*, and the focus of attention will be on the ultimate success of the project as a whole. Thus the revision of market demand estimates will lead to a prediction of the resulting impact on the new product's likely success and any necessary adjustment of plans for subsequent stages of the project.

(ii) To monitor the outputs achieved against desired outputs from time to time, and take whatever corrective action is necessary if a deviation exists. This is *feedback control*, and is illustrated in Figure 3.3.

As a hypothetical illustration, let us consider a company planning to sell 100 000 cassette players during the next 12 months. By the end of the third month it finds that

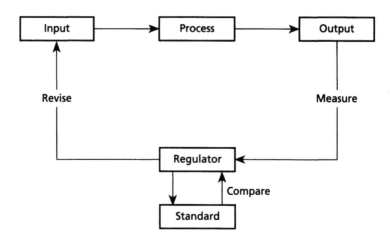

Figure 3.3 A feedback control system

the pattern of demand has fallen to an estimated 80 000 units for the 12 months due to the launch by another company of a competing product. After a further 3 months the competitor puts up the price of its product whilst the original company holds its own price steady, and this suggests that the annualized level of demand may increase to 150 000 units. Feedback signals would ensure that the company is made aware (e.g. by monthly reports) of the actual versus planned outcomes (in terms of sales levels). The launch of the competitive cassette player would be identified as the reason why sales levels were below expectations in the early months, and the competitor's price increase would be identified as the reason why sales levels subsequently increased. In response to deviations between actual and desired results (i.e. feedback) an explanation needs to be found, and actions taken to correct matters. Amending production plans to manufacture fewer (or more) cassette players, allowing inventory levels to fall (or rise) to meet the new pattern of demand, modifying promotional plans to counter competitive activities, and so forth, could all stem from a feedback control system.

If deviations (or *variances*, to give them their usual accounting name) are minor it is probable that the process could absorb them without any modifications, and inventory control systems, for example, are normally designed to accommodate minor variations between expected and actual levels of demand, with buffer stocks being held for this purpose. But in the case of extreme variations – such as the pattern of demand shifting from 100 000 units to 80 000 and then to 150 000 – it will be necessary to amend the inputs in a very deliberate way once the causes of the variations have been established. Inevitably there are costs associated with variances, and these will tend to be proportional to the length of time it takes to identify and correct them. (Variances are discussed in detail in Chapter 8.)

Both feedback and feedforward control entail linking outputs with other elements within the system, and this explains why they are termed *closed-loop* control systems.

(b) Closed-loop control

In an open-loop system errors cannot be corrected as the system goes along, whereas likely errors can be anticipated and steps taken to avoid them in a feedforward control system, and actual errors along the way can be identified and subsequent behaviour modified to achieve desired ends in a feedback control system.

The inadequacy of open-loop systems as a basis for organizational control (and hence for the design of managerial accounting systems) largely stems from our limited knowledge of how organizational systems operate, which in turn reflects the complexity of organizations and their environments, plus the uncertainty that clouds the likely outcomes of future events. If we possessed a full understanding of organizational processes and had a perfect ability to predict the future then we would be able to rely on open-loop systems to achieve the ends we desire since we would be able to plan with the secure knowledge that our plans would be attained due to our perfect awareness of what was going to happen, and how, and when (i.e. control action would be independent of the system's output).

In our current state of awareness we must rely on closed-loop systems, whether feedforward or feedback, in which control action is dependent upon the actual or anticipated state of the system.

It is helpful to think of four types of outcome in connection with the application of closed-loop systems to the problem of organizational control. These are:

S_0 = Initial *ex ante* performance (e.g. a budget based on a set of expectations, which might include, for instance, inflation at 5 per cent per annum; market growth of 10 per cent per annum; no labour disputes).

S_1 = Revised *ex ante* performance (e.g. an updated budget that has taken into account the experience of operating the system to date).

S_2 = *Ex post* performance (e.g. a revised budget based on what should have been achieved in the circumstances that prevailed during the period in question: say, inflation at 7 per cent per annum, market growth of 12 per cent per annum and a strike lasting three weeks).

A_0 = Observed performance (i.e. that which actually occurred).

An organization's forecasting ability is shown by $A_0 - S_0$ (under feedback control) and, more precisely, by $A_0 - S_1$ (under feedforward control). The extent to which the organization is not using its resources to maximum advantage (its opportunity cost of operating) is given by $A_0 - S_2$.

A feedforward control system will function in a way that keeps revising S_0 as events are proceeding with a view to producing an eventual outcome in which $A_0 = S_1$. On the other hand, a feedback control system will, from time to time, compare A_0 and S_0, and S_0 will only be revised if a discrepancy has been experienced.

It is apparent, therefore, that feedforward control tends to be:

- *ex ante*
- pro-active
- continuous

and seeks to predict the outcomes of proposed courses of action, while feedback control tends to be:

☐ *ex post*
☐ reactive
☐ episodic.

Let us look at each a little more closely.

(c) Feedforward control

A feedforward system can be defined as:

> A measurement and prediction system which assesses the system and predicts the output of the system at some future date.
>
> (Bhaskar and Housden 1985: 199)

This differs from a feedback system in that it seeks to anticipate, and thereby to avoid, deviations between actual and desired outcomes.

For a feedforward control system to be effective it must be based on a reasonably predictable relationship between inputs and outputs (i.e. there must be an adequate degree of understanding of the way in which the organization functions).

(d) Feedback control

Feedback control should ensure self-regulation in the face of changing circumstances once the control system has been designed and installed. The essence of feedback control is to be found in the idea of *homeostasis* which defines the process whereby key variables are maintained in a state of equilibrium even when there are environmental disturbances.

(e) Feedforward versus feedback control

The most significant features of feedforward and feedback control are shown in Figure 3.4. Feedback systems are typically cheaper and easier to implement than feedforward systems, and they are more effective in restoring a system that has gone out of control. Their main disadvantage, however, is that they can allow variations to persist for as long as it takes to detect and correct them. Feedforward control systems, as we have seen, depend critically for their effectiveness upon the forecasting ability of those who must predict future process outputs. Both feedforward and feedback systems lend themselves to self-regulation.

The most effective approach to control comes from using the two approaches as complements since few (if any) processes could be expected to operate effectively and efficiently for any length of time if only one type of control were in use. (For example, in controlling inventory, feedback data can be used in connection with stockouts, rates of usage, etc., while feedforward data needs to be generated in gauging stock requirements for predicted levels of demand and the ability of suppliers to deliver on time.)

Both types of control are fundamentally intertwined with the design of managerial accounting systems. In a feedback control system the functions that managerial accounting will carry out are:

Characteristic	Feedforward	Feedback
Low cost	—	Yes
Ease of implementation	—	Yes
Effectiveness	—	Yes
Minimal time delays	Yes	—
Self-regulation	Yes	Yes

Figure 3.4 Relative strengths of feedforward and feedback control
(Source: Adapted from Cushing 1982: 97)

☐ standard setting
☐ performance measurement
☐ reporting of results.

Within a feedforward control system the role of managerial accounting will encompass:

☐ standard setting
☐ monitoring process inputs
☐ monitoring operations
☐ predicting process outputs.

The degree of overlap is modest relative to the degree of complementarity.

Traditionally, accountants have focused on feedback information on outcomes. Thus, they measure outcome variables such as profitability, sales growth and production/activity level. In addition, although there is a tendency to emphasize the outcomes presumed to be desired by shareholders, management accountants also partly measure the outputs desired by other groups. For instance, there are some attempts to measure price for customers and wages for employees. Further, feedback information is also provided when the managerial accounting system provides information on the difference between actual and expected outcomes.

However, management accountants have not been as successful in the provision of feedforward information on inputs and outputs. This is partly because it is difficult to predict the future and to predict how an organization might interact with its external environment. Despite this, it appears that monitoring the environment will become more necessary as commercial organizations interact to a greater degree with other organizations and government regulatory agencies.

Finally, as already suggested, organizations should measure not only those outputs that are easy to quantify, but attempts should be made to measure all outputs that have a major impact on the organization.

3.3 CONTROL VERSUS CONTROLS

In the language of management the word 'controls' is not the plural of 'control'. Not only would it be wrong to assume that more 'controls' would automatically give us more 'control', it would be assuming they meant the same thing – which they do not.

'Controls' has the same meaning as measurement, or information, whereas 'control' is more akin to direction. 'Controls' is concerned with means whilst 'control' is concerned with ends, and they deal respectively with facts (i.e. events of the past) and expectations (i.e. desires about the future). From this it will be appreciated that 'controls' tend to be analytical and operational (concerning what was and what is), and 'control' tends to be normative (concerning what ought to be). A summary of key differences is shown in Figure 3.5.

The increasing ability, especially with the availability of computing power, to develop 'controls' has not necessarily increased our ability to 'control' organizations. If controls are to lead to control they must encourage human actors to behave in a way that facilitates adaptive behaviour on the part of the organization as a whole.

The complexity and uncertainty of the control problem are apparent when, for example, controls reveal that 'profits are falling'. But this does not indicate how one might (or should) respond – indeed, it would not be possible even to identify the whole array of potential responses! What is needed, therefore, if control is to be effective, is a basis for forming expectations about the future, as well as understanding about the past, that will enable us to combine these in order that we might behave in an adaptive way by either anticipating external changes and preparing to meet them, or by creating changes.

From this arises the basic question, 'How do we control?' In large part this is resolved by the answer to another question, 'What do we measure in order to control?' Care must be taken in measuring the key elements in any situation rather than those elements that lend themselves to easy measurement. ('Controls' are only helpful in 'control' if they are designed in the context of the overall control problem.)

Within business organizations many critical factors are either non-measurable or go unmeasured. For example, how does (or should) one measure the ability of an organization to attract or retain capable managers? This is more important to survival etc. than last year's reported profit, but it cannot be quantified even though it is

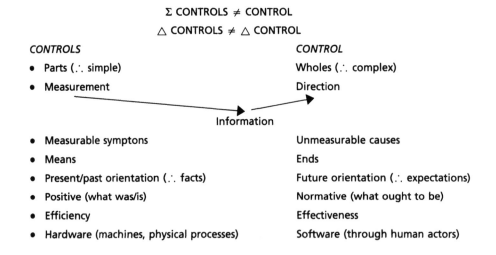

Figure 3.5 The different focus of control and controls

distinctly tangible. 'Controls' can only handle facts, i.e. observed events that are capable of measurement and quantification. There are no facts about the future, which is the temporal dimension of 'control', and there are many key control phenomena that are beyond our measuring competence. Furthermore, measurable facts are largely internal, whilst the environmental phenomena that give rise to the need for control are, by definition, external.

3.4 THE MARKETING CONTROLLER

If the controller is to execute his or her staff role satisfactorily for all areas of his or her organization he or she must become familiar with the nature of the various departments – engineering, R & D, marketing, manufacturing, logistics, etc. It is from the point of view of the operating managers located within these departments that the quality of the controller's service will be determined: if he or she is not supplying information that helps them to perform more effectively given their problems as they see them, then the controller in turn is not performing effectively. The link between information and action cannot be stressed too highly: the controller supplies the information, but if it is to lead to appropriate action it must be relevant to the circumstances within which the action must take place.

It will be apparent from the last paragraph that the idea of divisional or functional controllers is one that has frequently found favour in recent years. In a decentralized organization it is probable that a centralized controllership function will lack an adequate understanding of divisional activities, or that the controller's staff will not have empathy with the operating personnel. The outcome is likely to be a sub-optimal basis for effective control.

On the other hand, if each division has its own controller, there is a higher likelihood of a closer link between information and action. A variation on this theme that has not spread as widely as one might have anticipated, for reasons that are not wholly clear, is that of functional controllers. The idea of a marketing controller is well established, and the idea of a physical distribution controller also has support, with the holders of such posts being responsible for providing a planning and control information service for their functional superiors.

If one thinks about the reporting relationship between a divisional (or a functional) controller and, in the first place, his or her divisional superior and, in the second, his or her head-office superior, one sees the main inhibition to successfully employing this idea. A divisional controller cannot help having divided loyalties, and this puts him or her at risk in terms of being trusted and hence in terms of being effective in his or her divisional role.

However, technique is not the most critical ingredient in bringing management accounting into marketing in order to improve organizational effectiveness. The organization of the accounting function must be designed in the most appropriate way. One can envisage a range of alternative approaches to the marketing–accounting interface, such as:

1. no organized accounting support for marketing;
2. marketing accountants located within the accounting department;
3. marketing accountants located within the marketing department.

The whole reporting system can be strengthened by the existence of cost analysts within the marketing department. They would be responsible for preparing analyses for decision-making, such as associating costs with physical units rather than with the value of sales. This automatically eliminates any distortions arising from price variations.

Moreover, these analysts could secure uniformity in the measures used by marketing management and the controller's department – especially in relation to sales-force activities. Such measures might well include: cost per call, cost per customer, cost per order, break-even order size and sales per call. These measures could then shed light on profitability, workloads, sales quotas and compensation problems.

This is one means of securing closer coordination of the accounting and marketing functions which is so obviously desirable. The marketing manager's responsibility for profitability demands that there be a concern with costs and budgetary methods employed within the firm. It also demands an understanding of the way in which costs are built up and allocated to individual products; how budgets are arrived at; and how the services of the financial controller can best be employed to secure effective control and effective forward planning. Additionally, the marketing manager must appreciate the effect on profit of changes in the volume of production and should know the marginal earnings of each product (within the existing limits of production and organization). However, very few instances have been found in which the financial controller has combined the variable costs of both marketing and production at various volume levels for the use of the marketing team.

Progress from approach 1 to approach 3 is likely to be evolutionary as both functions learn about how best to interact, and time is also needed to develop the accounting systems whereby the marketing function may be assisted. But, above all, management accountants must acquire an understanding of the nature of marketing and the need to look outwards to the challenges of the environment.

The part that the financial controller can play in helping to control the marketing function is only gradually being accepted. The controller has, in fact, been looked upon with either suspicion or doubt as someone who only considered figures whereas marketing executives were convinced that people were more important. At best this made the controller a mere recorder of history – at worst, a positive barrier to progress.

Enlightenment will increase as the profit awareness of marketing management increases further, accompanied by an emphasis on the controller's service function. This service aspect of the controller's work requires that there should be a complete awareness of the firm's products, its markets, the marketing organization, and the particular problems that marketing management faces. Only when armed with this knowledge can the financial controller begin to develop the appropriate control and information systems.

3.5 SUMMARY

Within this chapter we have been concerned with the need for control in marketing and the characteristics of control in relation to the design of control systems.

Control was defined as a process involving anticipation and adaptation in relation to goal-striving behaviour. The discipline of cybernetics was used as a source of relevant concepts. Distinctions were drawn between open- and closed-loop control, and between feedforward and feedback control. It was suggested that the most effective control systems are designed using both feedforward and feedback principles.

Control (in the singular) was distinguished from *controls* (in the plural), and the point made that the latter need to be developed within a framework provided by the former.

The role of the financial controller in any organization is broad, given the pervasive nature of the financial dimension itself. A more focused role can be specified for a marketing controller. This needs to be considered in conjunction with the organizational location of such an individual if the needs of marketing specialists are to be best served.

Part 2

Feedforward Control

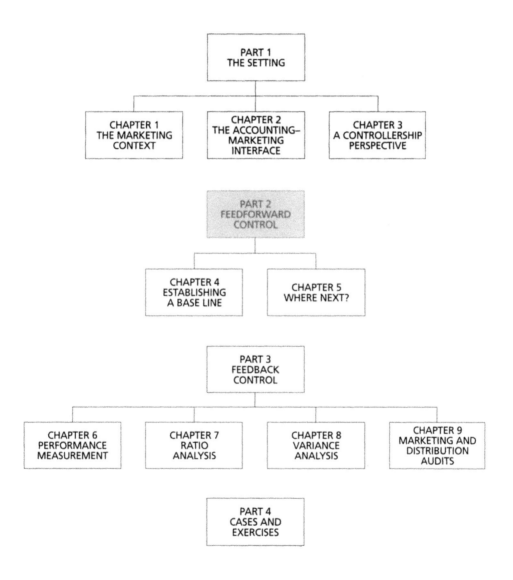

PART 1
THE SETTING

CHAPTER 1
THE MARKETING
CONTEXT

CHAPTER 2
THE ACCOUNTING–
MARKETING
INTERFACE

CHAPTER 3
A CONTROLLERSHIP
PERSPECTIVE

PART 2
FEEDFORWARD
CONTROL

CHAPTER 4
ESTABLISHING
A BASE LINE

CHAPTER 5
WHERE NEXT?

PART 3
FEEDBACK
CONTROL

CHAPTER 6
PERFORMANCE
MEASUREMENT

CHAPTER 7
RATIO
ANALYSIS

CHAPTER 8
VARIANCE
ANALYSIS

CHAPTER 9
MARKETING AND
DISTRIBUTION
AUDITS

PART 4
CASES AND
EXERCISES

Establishing a base line

4

LEARNING OBJECTIVES

After reading this chapter you should be able to:
- understand the principles of marketing cost analysis and how to apply these as a basis for feedforward control;
- appreciate the nature of marketing productivity and how this might be measured in the context of marketing segments;
- recognize the potential of Simmonds' approach to assessing competitive position.

4.1 INTRODUCTION

It is helpful in relation to the question 'How have resources been allocated within this organization?' to think of the organization as a bundle of projects or activities. This is relevant whether the organization is large or small, commercial or non-commercial, engaged in manufacturing or service rendering. Typical projects might be defined (as shown in Figure 5.1 on p. 69) along the following lines:

- reformulation and relaunch of product X;
- continued market success with product Y;
- the successful development and launch of product Z.

One might go further and define projects or activities in terms of missions: a mission represents the provision of a product or range of products at a particular level of service to a particular customer or customer group in a particular area. Figure 4.1 illustrates this.

An organization's mix of projects – or missions – will be constantly changing, and each has resource implications. For example, the scarcity of resources inevitably means that choices must be made in rationing available resources (whether in the form of funds, management time or whatever) between competing projects. It may be that new projects can only be adopted if old ones are deleted, thereby freeing resources. But how might a manager know which projects are worth retaining, which should be added to the portfolio, and which should be deleted? One starting point is to establish the cost of each of the organization's existing projects.

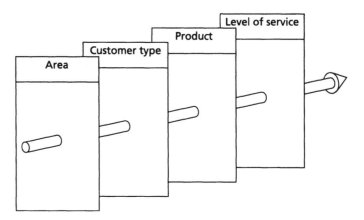

Figure 4.1 Multi-dimensional mission characteristics
(Source: Barrett 1980: 143)

We can think of cost as being equivalent in broad terms to effort, so what we are initially seeking to establish is how the available effort has been applied to the various activities in which the organization is engaged. This involves us in addressing the Stage One question in Figure 3.1 (see p. 26): 'Where are we now?' Once this has been answered it is possible to consider where to go next, and how (i.e. to proceed through Stages Two, Three and Four). Stage Five will be the subject of Part 3.

4.2 MARKETING COST ANALYSIS: AIMS AND METHODS

Control in marketing can be seen to be concerned with the allocation of total marketing effort to segments, along with the profitability of these allocations. It is generally found, however, that companies do not know the profitability of segments in marketing terms. Useful computations of marketing costs and profit contributions in the multi-product company require the adoption of analytical techniques that are not difficult in principle but are not widely adopted on account of, *inter alia*, the preoccupation with factory cost accounting that exists.

It is clearly essential for management to know the cost implications of different courses of action if the best is to be selected. In the pricing decision, for example, products may be priced in such a way as to give a specified rate of return. However, if costs are inappropriately allocated to products, then some products will be overpriced and some underpriced. (This is not intended to be an argument in favour of cost-plus pricing.)

The fact that most companies do not know what proportion of their total marketing outlay is spent on each product, area or customer group may be due to the absence of a sufficiently refined system of cost analysis, or it may be due to vagueness over the nature of certain costs. For instance, is the cost of packaging a promotional, a production or a distribution expense? Some important marketing costs are hidden in manufacturing costs or in general and administrative costs, including finished-goods inventory costs in the former and order-processing costs in the latter.

Since few companies are aware of costs and profits by segment in relation to sales levels, and since even fewer are able to predict changes in sales volume and profit contribution as a result of changes in marketing effort, the following errors arise:

1. Marketing budgets for individual products are too large, with the result that diminishing returns become evident and benefits would accrue from a reduction in expenditure.
2. Marketing budgets for individual products are too small and increasing returns would result from an increase in expenditure.
3. The marketing mix is inefficient, with an incorrect balance and incorrect amounts being spent on the constituent elements – such as too much on advertising and insufficient on direct selling activities.
4. Marketing efforts are misallocated amongst products and changes in these costs allocations (even with a constant level of overall expenditure) could bring improvements.

Similar arguments apply in relation to sales territories or customer groups as well as to products. The need exists, therefore, for control techniques to indicate the level of performance required and achieved as well as the outcome of shifting marketing efforts from one segment to another. As is to be expected, there exists great diversity in the methods by which manufacturers attempt to obtain costs (and profits) for segments of their business, but much of the cost data is inaccurate for such reasons as:

1. Order-getting costs may be allocated to individual products, sales areas, customer groups, etc., on the basis of sales value or sales volume, but this involves circular reasoning. Costs should be allocated in relation to causal factors, and it is order-getting expenditures that cause sales to be made rather than the other way round: managerial decisions determine order-getting costs. Furthermore, despite the fact that success is so often measured in terms of sales value achievements by product line, this basis fails to evaluate the efficiency of the effort needed to produce the realized sales value (or turnover). Even a seemingly high level of turnover for a specific product may really be a case of misallocated sales effort. (An example should make this clear: if a salesperson concentrates on selling product A which contributes £50 per hour of effort instead of selling product B which would contribute £120 per hour of effort, then it 'costs' the company £70 per hour spent on selling product A. This is the opportunity cost of doing one thing rather than another and is a measure of the sacrifice involved in selecting only one of several possible courses of action.)
2. General indirect and administrative costs are arbitrarily (and erroneously) allocated to segments on the basis of sales volume.
3. Many marketing costs are not allocated at all as marketing costs since they are not identified as such but are classified as manufacturing, general or administrative costs instead.

Marketing cost accounting (or analysis) has been developed to help overcome these problems and aims to:

1. Analyse the costs incurred in distributing and promoting products so that when they are combined with production cost data overall profitability can be determined.

2. Analyse the costs of marketing individual products to determine their profitability.
3. Analyse the costs involved in serving different classes of customers and different territories to determine their profitability.
4. Compute such figures as cost per sales call, cost per order, cost to put a new customer on the books, cost to hold £1's worth of inventory for a year, etc.
5. Evaluate managers according to their actual controllable cost responsibilities.
6. Evaluate alternative strategies or plans with a knowledge of full costs.

These analyses and evaluations provide senior management with the necessary information to enable them to decide which classes of customer to cultivate, which products to delete, which products to encourage, and so forth. Such analyses also provide a basis from which estimates can be made of the likely increases in product profitability that a specified increase in marketing effort should create. In the normal course of events it is far more difficult to predict the outcome of decisions that involve changes in marketing outlays in comparison with changes in production expenditure. It is easier, for instance, to estimate the effect of a new machine in the factory than it is to predict the impact of higher advertising outlays. Similarly, the effect on productive output of dropping a production worker is easier to estimate than is the effect on the level of sales caused by a reduction in the sales force.

The method of marketing cost analysis is similar to the method of product costing. Two stages are involved:

1. Marketing costs are initially reclassified from their *natural* expense headings (e.g. salaries) into *functional* cost groups (e.g. sales expenses) in such a way that each cost group brings together all the costs associated with a particular element of the marketing mix.
2. These functional cost groups are then apportioned to cost objects (e.g. products, customer groups, channels of distribution, etc.) on the basis of measurable criteria that bear a (proxy) causal relationship to the total amounts of the functional cost groups.

These two stages are illustrated in Figure 4.2.

Once the natural indirect expenses have been reclassified on a functional basis they are then charged to the segment in line with the usual benefit criterion (i.e. the segment is only allocated with that portion of each functional cost group that can be related to it on an imputed or proxy cause-and-effect basis). The logical basis of allocation may be apparent from an analysis of the underlying data, but it is important to observe that some costs vary with the characteristics of one type of segment only. Thus inventory costs depend on the characteristics of the products rather than on those of the customers, whereas the cost of credit depends on the financial integrity and number of customers rather than on regional factors. Accordingly, some functional costs should not be allocated to products, customers and territorial segments, but only to whichever segment or segments exhibit a (proxy) cause-and-effect relationship.

It must be remembered when using marketing cost analysis that any cost allocation involves a certain degree of arbitrariness which means that an element of error is inevitably contained within the allocation. Furthermore, it remains necessary to supplement the analysis of marketing costs with other relevant information and with managerial judgement.

Marketing cost analysis is the joint responsibility of the controller and the marketing manager, with the controller supplying most of the information and the marketing

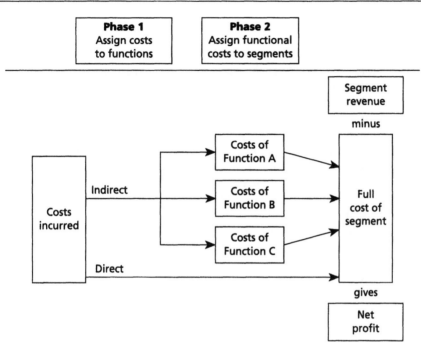

Figure 4.2 Determining segmental costs
(Source: Wilson and Chua 1993: 87)

manager supplying most of the judgement. Nevertheless, the marketing manager must be fully aware of the methods and limitations of marketing cost analysis. The high cost of establishing and maintaining a marketing costing system is justified by the benefits derived from increasing the efficiency of marketing effort. The risks involved in adopting marketing cost analysis before the benefits have been demonstrated can be reduced by initially confining the analysis to a sample of products, customers or territories, and by making periodic rather than continuous analyses.

Since a fundamental objective of marketing cost analysis lies in increasing the productivity of expenditures and not necessarily in their reduction the manager who wishes to introduce marketing cost analysis must emphasize the desire to make better use of existing resources rather than reduce future budgets. The integration of marketing costing with marketing research can assist in this matter. Confining any costing system to data provided from accounting records forces that system to be historical, but marketing research can provide estimates of future outcomes resulting from variations in marketing effort (with or without experimentation and the building of complex models) which enable the efficiency of alternative expenditure patterns to be predetermined and evaluated in accordance with corporate aims.

While costs can be broken down in a microscopic manner, there are dangers and limitations that should not be overlooked as they can hinder the control of marketing costs. If the outcome of functionalizing all marketing costs is to compute a unit cost for every activity, then this can be misleading. At the least a distinction should be made between fixed and variable costs, and the focus should be on the purpose for which a particular cost is to be derived and not simply on the means by which a figure is computed. Thus costs and units can be looked at separately, thereby avoiding myopic confusion.

An important distinction to make in marketing costs analysis – beyond the basic fixed–variable split – is that between separable fixed costs and non-separable fixed costs. A sales manager's salary is a fixed cost in conventional accounting, but in so far as his/her time can be linked to different products, sales territories, customers, etc., his/her salary (or at least portions of his/her salary) can be treated as being a separable fixed cost attributable to the segments in question in accordance with time devoted to each. In contrast, corporate advertising expenditure that is concerned with the company's image is not specific to any segment, hence it is non-separable and should not be allocated. Any non-specific, non-separable cost allocations would inevitably be very arbitrary, and such costs should therefore be excluded from all detailed cost and profit computations.

If one is concerned purely with measuring direct profit by segment, then separable fixed costs should be omitted from the calculations since they are not direct deductions from the sales revenue of specific segments. However, marketing cost analysis is concerned also with the most effective use of marketing effort, and this form of analysis can benefit from the inclusion of separable fixed costs. (This highlights an important difference between product costing and marketing cost analysis: the former is very much concerned with the task of simply compiling product costs whereas the latter is concerned with the cost and revenue implications of different marketing actions and activities.)

The financial control of marketing activities can now be seen to depend on the generation and analysis of information to attach costs and revenues realistically to the activities to which they relate. This in turn constitutes the basis on which the profit margin may be calculated – the size of which will tend to determine whether or not the activity under consideration is deemed satisfactory.

4.3 ILLUSTRATIONS OF SEGMENTAL ANALYSIS

In Figure 4.3 a number of segments are illustrated for a hypothetical engineering company, XYZ Ltd. It is possible to measure the costs and revenues at each level in order to highlight the profit performance of each segment. Thus, for example, the profit performance for the calculator market may be measured along the lines shown in Figure 4.4.

The approach adopted in Figure 4.4 is a *contribution* approach, with costs and revenues being assigned to segments on bases that are essentially direct. Common costs have not been assigned to segments at all.

Although the contribution approach avoids the controversies surrounding the apportionment of indirect costs to segments there can be benefits in carrying out apportionments – provided the bases are clearly thought out and have a (proxy) causal connection with cost levels. This approach gives the foundation of *marketing productivity analysis*.

The nature of productivity

Productivity can be considered at either a macro level (i.e. in relation to entire industries or whole economies) or at a micro level (i.e. in relation to particular

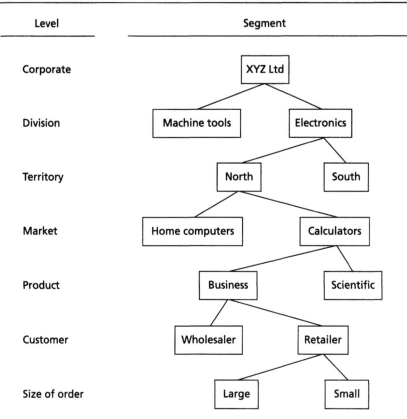

Figure 4.3 Segmental levels
(Source: adapted from Ratnatunga 1983: 34)

organizations, or in relation to particular activities within organizations). Our interest is in the latter – productivity at a micro level – although we must avoid being too introspective by focusing exclusively on one organization or function as if it were independent of its context.

At its simplest, productivity can be conceived of as the relationship between outputs and inputs. Thus marketing productivity can be expressed as:

$$\frac{\text{marketing outputs}}{\text{marketing inputs}}$$

Sevin (1965: 9) has defined marketing productivity in more specific terms as

> the ratio of sales or net profits (effect produced) to marketing costs (energy expended) for a specific segment of the business.

This equates productivity and profitability, which seems acceptable to some writers (e.g. Thomas 1984, 1986) but not to others (e.g. Bucklin 1978). The major objection to Sevin's definition is due to the effects of inflation since sales revenue, net profit and costs are all financial flows subject to changes in relative prices. For example, any

Product: Calculators	North territory (£)	South territory (£)	Total (£)
Net sales	xxx	xxx	xxxx
Variable manufacturing costs	xx	xx	xxx
Manufacturing contribution	xx	xx	xxx
Marketing costs			
Variable:			
Sales commissions	x	x	x
Selling expenses	x	x	x
Variable contribution	xx	xx	xxx
Assignable:			
Salespersons' salaries	x	x	x
Manager's salary	x	x	x
Product advertising	x	x	x
Product contribution	xx	xx	xx
Non-assignable:			
Corporate advertising			x
Marketing contribution			xx
Fixed common costs:			
Manufacturing			x
Administration			x
Net profit			xx

Figure 4.4 Segmental contribution statement

increase in the value of sales from one period to another during inflationary times will be made up of two elements:

☐ an increase due to a higher physical volume of sales;
☐ an increase due to higher prices.

If the value of the pound sterling were constant this would remove the problem, but since this is not the case it means that any financial data is necessarily suspect. The answer is to make some adjustments to ensure that measurement is made in real terms rather than simply in monetary terms – and to make these adjustments to both numerator and denominator in a way that allows for differential rates of inflation. Once measurement is made in real terms it is possible to use the ratio that emerges as an index of efficiency. This can be used in relation to two types of question:

☐ How much output was achieved for a given input?
☐ How much input was required to achieve a given output?

These questions can be asked retrospectively (as above) or prospectively (for example, how much output should be achieved from a given mix and quantity of inputs?). The first relates to the notion of *technical* efficiency, whereby one seeks to maximize the output from a given input, whereas the second relates to the notion of *economic* efficiency, whereby one seeks to minimize the input costs for a given output.

Having specified in operational terms the numerator (output) and the denominator (input), and having eliminated the impacts of inflation, the result represents a measure of resource allocation (i.e. the pattern of inputs) and resource utilization (i.e. the generation of outputs), and these can be depicted via ratio pyramids which we will look at in Chapter 7 (see pp. 98–103). What we need to recognize at this point is that the array of ratios within a ratio pyramid can give us a vivid picture of the manner in which the organization has allocated its resources and the efficiency with which those resources have been utilized. The next step, of course, is to consider how the allocation and its efficiency might be improved, which will mean changes in inputs and outputs. In turn this requires an understanding of the causal relationships between inputs and outputs.

Let us be a little more specific and consider a particular productivity index from the distribution domain. The relevant output may be expressed in terms of the number of orders shipped during a given period, and the associated input may be the number of distribution labour hours worked in the period. Thus:

$$\text{productivity index} = \frac{\text{number of orders shipped}}{\text{number of distribution labour hours worked}}$$

It will be apparent that this index relates one physical measure to another, and hence there is no need to worry about inflationary distortions. However, had the numerator been expressed in terms of the sales value of orders shipped and the denominator in terms of the cost of distribution labour hours worked, it would have been necessary to adjust the figures to eliminate the effects of inflation – even though the index that results is a true ratio (i.e. it is not stated in terms of specific units).

It should also be apparent that any productivity index that is calculated is meaningless in isolation of some comparative figure. With what should an index be compared? There are a number of alternatives that will be examined later in more detail, but for the present we should be aware of the following:

☐ Internal comparisons can be made with either
  – figures from previous periods, which give a basis for trend analysis;
  – figures representing efficient or desired performance, which give a basis for budgetary control.
☐ External comparisons can be made with other organizations operating within the same markets.

The importance of external reference points cannot be over emphasized. As Christopher (1977) has stated:

> Business success is achieved where the client is, more than in our plants. External returns from the market are more appropriate measures than internal returns on investment. Success is more in manufacturing satisfied, repeat customers than in manufacturing products.

Within the distribution domain it has been estimated that order-filling activities (i.e. transportation, stockholding and associated administration) account for between 18 and 45 per cent of total company costs. Outlays of this magnitude clearly warrant attention.

The steps to be followed in carrying out productivity analyses were hinted at in the section starting on p. 42. They are:

1. determine the analysis to be made (i.e. specific segments);
2. classify costs into appropriate categories (as discussed in the section starting on p. 42);
3. select bases for apportioning indirect costs to functional activities;
4. allocate revenue and direct costs to the chosen segment;
5. apply indirect costs to the segment;
6. summarize steps 4 and 5 into a statement showing the net profit of the segment;
7. interpret the results from step 6.

ABC Ltd: an exercise on segmental analysis

An example is given in Figure 4.5 of the net profit picture in an organization operating through three different channels of distribution.

The net profit figure reflects the result of the allocation of effort as shown by the total of:

☐ cost of goods sold
☐ direct expenses
☐ indirect expenses

once this allocation has been set against the revenue figure, channel by channel. It is evident that the validity of the net profit figures that emerge depends critically upon the adequacy of the means by which indirect costs are apportioned.

The following example illustrates in detail how the above approach might be implemented.

£'000s

	Channel			
	A	B	C	Total
Revenue	875	950	1,225	3,050
Cost of goods sold	325	285	490	1,100
Gross profit	550	665	735	1,950
Direct expenses	265	245	450	960
Indirect expenses	330	275	250	855
	595	520	700	1,815
Net profit	(45)	145	35	135

Figure 4.5 Profit analysis by channel

	£
Sales revenue	255,000
Cost of goods sold	178,500
Gross profit	76,500

Expenses	£	
Salaries	37,500	
Rent	7,500	
Packaging materials	15,180	
Postage and stationery	750	
Hire of office equipment	1,500	
		62,430
Net profit		£14,070

Figure 4.6 Profit and loss account for ABC Ltd

The profit and loss account for last month's operations of ABC Ltd is given in Figure 4.6, showing a net profit of £14,070. Derek Needham, ABC's chief executive, is interested in knowing the net profit made from each of the company's three customers. Since this cannot be known from Figure 4.6 as it stands, he asks his management accountant, Philip Randall, to carry out the necessary analysis.

In addition to the five *natural* accounts shown in the profit and loss account Mr Randall has identified four *functional* accounts:

☐ personal selling
☐ packaging and despatch
☐ advertising
☐ invoicing and collection.

His investigations have revealed that:

1. Salaries are attributable as follows:
   ☐ Sales personnel   £15,000
   ☐ Packaging labour   £13,500
   ☐ Office staff   £9,000.
   Sales staff seldom visit the office. Office staff time is divided equally between promotional activities on the one hand and invoicing/collecting on the other.
2. The rent charge relates to the whole building, of which 20 per cent is occupied by offices and the remainder by packaging/despatch.
3. All the advertising expenditure is related to product C.
4. ABC Ltd markets three products, as shown in Figure 4.7. These products vary in their manufactured cost (worked out on absorption lines), selling price, and volume sold during the month. Moreover, their relative bulk varies: product A is much smaller than product B, which in turn is only half the size of product C. Details are given in Figure 4.7.

Product	Manufactured cost per unit	Selling price per unit	Number of units sold last month	Sales revenue	Relative bulk per unit
A	£105	£150	1,000	£150,000	1
B	£525	£750	100	£75,000	3
C	£2,100	£3,000	10	£30,000	6
			1,110	£255,000	

Figure 4.7 ABC Ltd: basic product data

Customer	Number of sales calls in period	Number of orders placed in period	Number of units of each product ordered in period		
			A	B	C
Charles	30	30	900	30	0
James	40	3	90	30	3
Hugh	30	1	10	40	7
Totals	100	34	1000	100	10

Figure 4.8 ABC Ltd: basic customer data

5. Each of ABC's three customers requires different product combinations, places a different number of orders and requires a different amount of sales effort. As Figure 4.8 shows, James received more sales calls, Charles placed more orders and Hugh made up most of the demand for product C.

Using the data that has been presented, and making any assumptions we feel to be appropriate, we can apply absorption costing principles in order to determine the net profit or loss attributable to each of ABC's customers.

On the basis of our calculations we can consider alternative courses of action. We can proceed in the following manner:

(a) Analysis of data

Among the given data we are told that office staff divide their time equally between two functional activities:

☐ advertising (i.e. order-getting)
☐ invoicing and collections.

It seems reasonable to assume (in the absence of other guidance) that space, postage and stationery, and office equipment are used equally by these two functions. The calculations that follow are based on this assumption, but any other reasonable (and explicit) basis could be acceptable.

Product	Number of units sold		Relative bulk per unit		Packaging units
A	1000	×	1	=	1000
B	100	×	3	=	300
C	10	×	6	=	60
	1110				1360

Figure 4.9 ABC Ltd: packaging units

Natural expense	Personal selling	Packaging and despatch	Advertising	Invoicing and collection
Salaries	£15,000	£13,500	£4,500	£4,500
Rent	—	£6,000	£750	£750
Packaging materials	—	£15,180	—	—
Postage and stationery	—	—	£375	£375
Hire of equipment	—	—	£750	£750
Total	£15,000	£34,680	£6,375	£6,375

Figure 4.10 ABC Ltd: assigning natural expenses

Rent is payable on the basis of:

☐ 20 per cent office space (i.e. £1,500);
☐ 80 per cent packaging and despatch space (i.e. £6,000).

All packaging materials are chargeable to packaging and despatch (which is a clear-cut example of a direct functional cost). Since packaging costs will vary with the bulk of the products sold rather than with, say, the number of units sold or sales revenue, we need to take note of the causal relationship between the bulk of sales and packaging costs (see Figure 4.9).

This can be done by computing (as in Figure 4.9) a measure termed 'packaging units' which incorporates both the number of units and their relative bulk. Even though only 10 units of product C are sold during the month the relative bulk of that product (with a factor of 6) ensures that it uses a correspondingly high amount of packaging effort (hence cost) per unit relative to products A and B.

The bases for determining the rates to apply functional costs to segments can be built up in the following way:

(i) *Assign natural expenses to functional activities.* This is done in Figure 4.10.
(ii) *Select bases for assigning functional costs to segments.*
    ☐ Sales calls can be used for personal selling expenses (although this assumes all calls took an equal amount of time).
    ☐ The packaging costs vary in accordance with the number of packaging units handled, so a rate per product can be established by taking bulk and the number of units handled into account.

☐ Advertising can be related to the number of units of product C sold during the period (which assumes that advertising was equally effective for all sales and that all its benefits were obtained during the period in question).

☐ The costs of invoicing can be assumed to vary in accordance with the number of orders (hence invoices) processed during the period.

Relevant calculations are as follows:

$$\text{Cost per sales call} = \frac{\text{Functional costs}}{\text{No. of sales calls}} = \frac{£15,000}{100} = £150.00$$

$$\text{Packaging costs} = \frac{\text{Functional costs}}{\text{No. of packaging units}} = \frac{£34,680}{1,360} = £25.50$$

$$\text{Product A} = £25.50 \times 1 = £25.50$$

$$\text{Product B} = £25.50 \times 3 = £76.50$$

$$\text{Product C} = £25.50 \times 6 = £153.00$$

$$\text{Advertising cost} = \frac{\text{Functional costs}}{\text{Units of C sold}} = \frac{6,375}{10} = £637.50$$

$$\text{Invoicing cost per order} = \frac{\text{Functional costs}}{\text{No. of orders}} = \frac{£6,375}{34} = £187.50$$

(iii) *Assign functional costs to segments.* Before this step can be executed fully it is necessary to calculate the cost of goods sold (COGS) on a customer-by-customer basis. Data in Figure 4.7 include the manufactured cost per unit of each product, and from Figure 4.8 we can see how many units of each product are bought by each customer. From this we can calculate the data in Figure 4.11.

We can now turn to the assigning of functional costs to segments. If we take the case of Charles we know what he can be attributed with (see Figure 4.12).

A similar computation needs to be carried out for James and Hugh, which gives us the data in Figure 4.13.

Finally, the revenue generated from each customer must be calculated as in Figure 4.14.

Product	Unit cost of goods sold	Customer					
		Charles		James		Hugh	
		Units	COGS	Units	COGS	Units	COGS
A	£105	900	94,500	90	9,450	10	1,050
B	£525	30	15,750	30	15,750	40	21,000
C	£2,100	0	0	3	6,300	7	14,700
			£110,250		£31,500		£36,750

Figure 4.11 ABC Ltd: assigning functional expenses

	Charles	
30 sales calls	@ £150.00	£4,500
30 orders	@ £187.50	£5,625
Packaging costs for:		
Product A 900 × £25.50	£22,950.00	
Product B 30 × £76.50	£2,295.00	
Product C 0 × £153.00	0	
		£25,245
Advertising		0
Segmental marketing cost		£35,370

Figure 4.12 ABC Ltd: Charles' costs

James			Hugh		
40 sales calls @ £150.00	£6,000.00		30 sales calls @ £150.00	£4,500.00	
3 orders @ £187.50	£562.50		1 order @ £187.50	£187.50	
Packaging			Packaging		
A 90 × £25.50 £2,295			A 10 × £25.50 £255		
B 30 × £76.50 £2,295			B 40 × £76.50 £3,060		
C 3 × £153.0 £459			C 7 × £153.00 £1,071		
	£5,049.00			£4,386.00	
Advertising 3 × £637.50	£1,912.50		Advertising 7 × £637.00	£4,462.50	
Segmental marketing cost	£13,524.00		Segmental marketing cost	£13,536.00	

Figure 4.13 ABC Ltd: costs of James and Hugh

Product	Unit selling price (£)	Customer					
		Charles		James		Hugh	
		Units	Revenue	Units	Revenue	Units	Revenue
A	150	900	135,000	90	13,400	10	1,500
B	740	30	22,500	30	22,500	40	30,000
C	3,000	0	0	3	9,000	7	21,000
			£157,500		£45,000		£52,500

Figure 4.14 ABC Ltd: revenue by customer

(iv) *Compile a net profit statement.* All the pieces can now be put together to show the profit or loss of each customer account with ABC Ltd. The resulting figures (Figure 4.15) show that Charles' and Hugh's are profitable accounts while James' is marginally unprofitable.

	Customer			
	Charles	*James*	*Hugh*	*ABC Ltd*
Sales revenue	£157,500	£45,000	£52,500	£255,000
Cost of goods sold	110,250	31,500	36,750	178,500
Gross profit	47,250	13,500	15,750	178,500
Marketing expenses	35,370	13,524	13,536	62,430
Net profit	£11,880	£(24)	£2,214	£14,070

Figure 4.15 ABC Ltd: net profit by customer

In productivity terms we have:

Charles: $\dfrac{\text{Outputs}}{\text{Inputs}} = \dfrac{£157,000}{£(110,250 + 35,370)} = 1.08$

James: $\dfrac{\text{Outputs}}{\text{Inputs}} = \dfrac{£45,000}{£(31,500 + 13,524)} = 0.99$

Hugh: $\dfrac{\text{Outputs}}{\text{Inputs}} = \dfrac{£52,000}{£(36,750 + 13,536)} = 1.04$

ABC Ltd: $\dfrac{\text{Outputs}}{\text{Inputs}} = \dfrac{£225,000}{£(178,500 + 62,430)} = 1.06$

(b) Interpretation of data

A danger in using an absorption-based approach in segmental analysis is that the 'bottom line' might be taken as a criterion for *action*. It should not be: the aim is to determine the net profit as a criterion for *investigation*. (In a sense, of course, this is one type of action, but the type of action that should be avoided is the eliminating of James' account due to the marginal loss revealed in Figure 4.15).

Charles's account contributed almost 85 per cent of the total net profit, and he bought three times as much from ABC Ltd as did Hugh, and more than three times the purchases of James. However, the number of sales calls to Charles was fewer than to James, although Charles placed a much larger number of orders than both James and Hugh together.

The mix of products purchased clearly affects the profit performance of different customer accounts. While the cost of goods sold does not vary from one product to another (being 70 per cent of sales revenue for each product line), the variation in relative bulk of the product lines causes differences in packaging costs. Thus Charles (whose orders were for 900 units of A, 30 of B, and none of C) was charged with relatively less packaging cost than either James or Hugh due to the smaller packaging bulk of product A. On a similar basis, since Charles bought no units of C his account was not charged with any advertising costs, so the profit performance of Charles' account would clearly be better than either of the others.

One possible way forward could be to consider calling less often on James, encourage Charles to place fewer (but larger) orders, and to rethink the wisdom of the advertising campaign for product C.

It is vital to recognize that this net profit approach to segmental analysis can only raise questions regarding possible future actions; it cannot provide any answers. (The reason for this, of course, is that the apportionment of indirect costs clouds the distinction between avoidable and unavoidable costs, and even direct costs may not be avoidable in the short run.)

The application of the above steps to a company's product range may produce the situation portrayed in Figure 4.6.

The segment could equally be sales territory, customer group, etc., and after the basic profit computation has been carried out it can be supplemented (as in Figure 4.17) by linking it to an analysis of the effort required to produce the profit result. (Clearly this is a multivariate situation, as indicated in Figure 4.17 above, in which profit depends upon a variety of input factors, but developing valid and reliable multivariate models is both complex and expensive. As a step in the direction of more rigorous analysis one can derive benefits from linking profit outcomes to individual inputs – such as selling time in the case of Figure 4.17.)

From Figure 4.17 one can see that product A generates 43.7 per cent of total profits, requiring only 16.9 per cent of available selling time. This is highly productive. By contrast, product E produces only 6.8 per cent of total profits but required 10.2 per cent of selling effort. Even worse, however, is the 24.8 per cent of selling effort devoted to products G and H which are unprofitable.

A number of obvious questions arise from this type of analysis. Can the productivity of marketing activities be increased by:

1. increasing net profits proportionately more than the corresponding increase in marketing outlays?
2. increasing net profits with no change in marketing outlays?
3. increasing net profits with a decrease in marketing costs?
4. maintaining net profits at a given level but decreasing marketing costs?
5. decreasing net profits but with a proportionately greater decrease in marketing costs?

If these analyses are based purely on historical information they will provide less help than if they relate to plans for the future. One way of overcoming the limitations of historical information is to plan and control the conditions under which information is gathered. This can be achieved through *marketing experimentation* (see Chapter 5).

4.4 SIMMONDS' APPROACH

Another approach to addressing the question 'Where are we now?' is provided by Simmonds (1986), who sought to assess an enterprise's competitive position. He deserves the credit for developing *strategic management accounting*, which he defined (1981a) as:

Product	% contribution to total profits
Total for all products	100.00
Profitable products:	
A	43.7
B	35.5
C	16.4
D	9.6
E	6.8
F	4.2
Sub-total	116.2
Unprofitable products:	
G	−7.5
H	−8.7
Sub-total	−16.2

Figure 4.16 Segmental profit statement

Product	% contribution to total profits	% total selling time
Total for all products	100	100
Profitable products:		
A	43.7	16.9
B	35.5	18.3
C	16.4	17.4
D	9.6	5.3
E	6.8	10.2
F	4.2	7.1
Sub-total	116.2	75.2
Unprofitable products:		
G	−7.5	9.5
H	−8.7	15.3
Sub-total	−16.2	24.8

Figure 4.17 Segmental productivity statement

The provision and analysis of management accounting data about a business and its competitors for use in developing and monitoring the business strategy.

He emphasizes the particular importance of relative levels and trends in:

☐ real costs and prices
☐ volume

☐ market share
☐ cash flow
☐ the proportion demanded of an enterprise's total resources.

The key notion here is that of an enterprise's position *relative to* competitors' positions. Insofar as strategy is concerned with competitive position it has been largely ignored by management accountants, but in a number of papers Simmonds (1981a, 1982, 1985, 1986) proposed how this failing might be overcome.

A basic plank in his argument is the preoccupation that accountants have with the recording, analysing and presentation of cost data relating to existing activities. This 'data orientation' begs some fundamental questions – such as why the data are being collected in the first place. An alternative, and preferable, approach is one of 'information orientation' which starts with the diagnosis of problems, leading to the structuring of decisions, and thence to the specification of information that will help in making appropriate decisions. The focus shifts from the analysis of costs *per se* to the value of information.

The manager wishing to make decisions that will safeguard his or her organization's strategic position must know by whom, by how much, and why he or she is gaining or being beaten. In other words, strategic indicators of performance are required. Conventional measures, such as profit, will not suffice.

Let us take comparative costs as a starting point. It is intuitively the case that organizations having a cost advantage (i.e. lower unit cost for a product of comparable specification) are strong and those having a cost disadvantage are weak. If we relate this to the idea of the experience curve it will be appreciated that, if costs can be made to decline predictably with cumulative output, the enterprise that has produced most should have the lowest unit cost and, therefore, the highest profits.

Apart from cost an enterprise may seek to gain competitive advantage via its pricing policy. In this setting the management accountant can attempt to assess each major competitor's cost structure and relate this to their prices – taking care to eliminate the effects of inflation from the figures being used. Applying cost–volume–profit analysis to one's competitors is likely to be more fruitful than simply applying it internally.

> Clearly, competitor reactions can substantially influence the outcome of a price move. Moreover, likely reactions may not be self-evident when each competitor faces a different cost–volume–profit situation. Competitors may not follow a price lead nor even march in perfect step as they each act to defend or build their own positions. For an adequate assessment of the likelihood of competitor price reactions, then, some calculation is needed of the impact of possible price moves on the performance of individual competitors. Such an assessment in turn requires an accounting approach that can depict both competitor cost–volume–profit situations and their financial resources.
>
> (Simmonds 1982: 207)

After dealing with costs and prices the next important (and related) variable to consider is volume – especially market share. By monitoring movements in market share an enterprise can see whether it is gaining or losing position, and an examination of relative market shares will indicate the strengths of different competitors.

Reporting market share details along with financial details can help in making managerial accounting reports more strategically relevant.

The significance of competitive position has been highlighted by Simmonds (1986) as being the basic determinant of future profits and of the business's value. Moreover, since competitive position can change over time, so can profits and value, but it should not be assumed that an improvement in competitive position will be associated with an improvement in short-run profits. In fact, the opposite is likely to be the case due to the need to incur costs in building up a competitive position, which has the effect of depressing current profits in favour of future profits. This raises the question as to whether competitive position can be measured in accounting terms – not just for a given business but also for its main competitors, and not just at a point in time but also over time. Simmonds has attempted to do this by applying strategic management accounting. He makes it clear, however, that it is not possible to express competitive position as a single figure. Instead it is possible to offer an array of indicators relating to the competitive situation. From these indicators managers can gain insights into a business's competitive position which will help them in judging whether or not things are moving in their favour.

Simmonds recommends that competitive data be built up for the market leader, close competitors and laggards rather than for all competitors. The following data might most usefully be developed. (The example that follows is derived from that given in Simmonds (1986) and is used with permission).

(a) Sales and market share

Sales revenue of each firm relative to the total market is a cornerstone, and changes in market share should be closely monitored. A decrease in market share suggests a loss of competitive position, with unfortunate implications for future profits. Conversely, an increase in market share suggests an improved competitive position with the prospect of improved future profits. By adding market share details to management accounting reports managers are able to make much more sense of what is happening.

Figure 4.18 gives sales and market share data for Firm A and the total market for Product X. We can see that, despite an increase in sales revenue of 20 per cent for Firm A, the market share has slipped from 19 to 16 per cent. This is explained by the growth in the total market of 44 per cent. It seems probable that the firm's failure to keep pace with the overall market growth will be reflected in a poorer competitive

	Firm A	Total market
Sales (£'000)		
Last year	1,000	5,200
This year	1,200	7,500
% change	+20	+44
Market share (%)		
Last year	19	100
This year	16	100

Figure 4.18 Sales and market share data, Product X

	Sales (£'000s)	Market share (%)	Relative market share
Total market:			
Last year	5,200		
This year	7,500		
Firm A:			
Last year	1,000	19	
This year	1,200	16	
Leading competitor:			
Last year	2,200	42	2.20
This year	3,600	48	3.00
Close competitor:			
Last year	1,200	23	1.20
This year	2,000	27	1.67

Figure 4.19 Relative market shares

position: not only might competitors have gained market share at the firm's expense, but this is likely to be accompanied by cost advantages and hence improved profits. Some details are given in Figure 4.19.

Relative market share is calculated by dividing each competitor's market share by that of one's own firm, and it indicates any gains or losses. As Figure 4.19 makes clear, Firm A has slipped relative to both the market leader and its closest competitor. The leader's market share has increased to three times that of Firm A, and will almost certainly have lowered its unit costs.

(b) Profits and return on sales

If a competitor has a higher return on sales than Firm A it may well reduce price, or improve quality, or increase its marketing efforts in order to improve its competitive position further.

The data in Figure 4.20 show sales, market share, relative market share, and profit (before tax but after interest) over the last three years for all firms supplying Product X. Over that period the market leader's profit has grown by 400 per cent, the closest competitor's by over 200 per cent, and Firm A's by only 90 per cent. In absolute terms the market leader's profit in year 3 is almost five times that of Firm A, giving a huge source of funds for expansion, R & D, etc., whilst in relative terms the leader's return on sales of 22.2 per cent in year 3 is well ahead of any other competitor.

Firm A's task seems to be both to reinforce its competitive position relative to laggard firms and to develop a defence against the strong competitors.

(c) Volume and unit cost

Details of volume and costs are given in Figure 4.21. Changes in unit costs reveal each firm's relative efficiency: the further a competitor's relative cost falls below unity the more of a threat this becomes, and vice versa. (Costs are calculated by subtracting

	Sales (£'000s)	Market share (%)	Relative market share	Profit (£'000s)	(%)
Firm A:					
Year 1	700	17.5		90	12.8
Year 2	1,000	19.2		130	13.0
Year 3	1,200	16.0		170	14.2
Leading competitor:					
Year 1	1,400	35.0	2.0	200	14.3
Year 2	2,200	42.3	2.2	400	18.2
Year 3	3,600	48.0	3.0	800	22.2
Close competitor:					
Year 1	1,000	25.0	1.4	120	12.0
Year 2	1,200	23.1	1.2	170	14.2
Year 3	2,000	26.6	1.7	260	13.0
Laggard 1:					
Year 1	500	12.5	0.71	55	11.0
Year 2	500	9.6	0.50	60	12.0
Year 3	500	6.7	0.42	50	10.0
Laggard 2:					
Year 1	400	10.0	0.57	40	10.0
Year 2	300	5.8	0.30	20	6.7
Year 3	200	2.7	0.17	5	2.5
Total market:					
Year 1	4,000	100.0		505	12.6
Year 2	5,200	100.0		780	15.0
Year 3	7,500	100.0		1,285	17.1

Figure 4.20 Sales, market shares and profits for all suppliers of Product X

profit from sales revenue, and unit costs are obtained by dividing the costs by volume, year by year.)

The market leader has a cost advantage in year 3 of 69p per unit relative to Firm A, whereas Laggard 2 has a cost disadvantage relative to Firm A of 73p per unit. Perhaps more significant than these figures are those that compare volume and cost changes. Thus, for example, Firm A's two main competitors both increased volume between years 2 and 3 by more than 70 per cent, yet the close competitor's cost per unit only fell by 3 per cent or so whilst the market leader's cost per unit fell by more than 9 per cent. Is the explanation to be found in the close competitor's investment in competitive position – such as in R & D, marketing programmes or new plant?

(d) Unit prices

In Figure 4.22 are shown the unit prices charged for product X by each competitor over the last three years, along with costs and the profits and market shares that

	Volume in units (000s)	Increase (%)	Cost (£'000s)	Cost per unit (£)	Relative cost per unit
Firm A:					
Year 1	100		610	6.10	
Year 2	156	56	870	5.58	
Year 3	192	23	1,030	5.36	
Leading competitor:					
Year 1	200		1,200	6.00	0.98
Year 2	350	75	1,800	5.14	0.92
Year 3	600	71	2,800	4.67	0.87
Close competitor:					
Year 1	140		880	6.29	1.03
Year 2	190	36	1,030	5.42	0.97
Year 3	330	74	1,740	5.27	0.98
Laggard 1:					
Year 1	70		445	6.36	1.04
Year 2	75	7	440	5.86	1.05
Year 3	80	7	450	5.62	1.05
Laggard 2:					
Year 1	56		360	6.42	1.05
Year 2	45	(20)	280	6.22	1.16
Year 3	32	(29)	195	6.09	1.14
Total:					
Year 1	566				
Year 2	816	44			
Year 3	1,234	51			

Figure 4.21 Volume, costs and unit costs

have resulted. (Unit prices are simply calculated by dividing sales revenue by units sold.)

The pattern of price changes reflects the use of price as a competitive variable, and this can be related to cost and market share data to see how competitive positions are changing. For example, the market leader has reduced the price by more than any other firm, but its price reductions have not been as great as its cost reductions, hence profit per unit has increased each year – as has the number of units sold. This places that firm in a very strong competitive position.

Patterns of price, cost, profit and volume change for Firm A and its closest competitor are less clear, but for the laggards the picture of a downward spiral is clear enough.

(e) Cash flow, liquidity and resource availability

Competitive gains and losses will arise over longer periods than the financial year, and the capacity of a competitor to continue in the fray is a function of more than

	Average price per unit (£)	Average cost per unit (£)	Profit per unit (£)	Market share (%)
Firm A:				
Year 1	7.00	6.10	0.90	17.5
Year 2	6.41	5.58	0.83	19.2
Year 3	6.25	5.36	0.89	16.0
Leading competitor:				
Year 1	7.00	6.00	1.00	35.0
Year 2	6.29	5.14	1.15	42.3
Year 3	6.00	4.67	1.33	48.0
Close competitor:				
Year 1	7.14	6.29	0.85	25.0
Year 2	6.31	5.42	0.89	23.1
Year 3	6.06	5.27	0.79	26.6
Laggard 1:				
Year 1	7.14	6.36	0.78	12.5
Year 2	6.66	5.86	0.80	9.6
Year 3	6.25	5.62	0.63	6.7
Laggard 2:				
Year 1	7.14	6.42	0.72	10.0
Year 2	6.66	6.22	0.44	5.8
Year 3	6.25	6.09	0.16	2.7

Figure 4.22 Unit prices, profits and market shares

simply profit or market share at a particular point in time. A firm's ability to continue to compete will also depend upon its liquidity position and the availability of other resources over time. For example, a firm with poor cash flow, a high level of debt and out-of-date production facilities is not likely to be able to compete for long.

(f) The Future

Having analysed the relative positions of each firm supplying product X over the past three years the real crunch comes in attempting to make the next move.

The management of Firm A will be able to see that the market leader is controlling the competitive situation with the highest volume and profits, along with the lowest unit costs and price. If that firm reduced its price by, say, 10 per cent it would force the laggards out of the market and limit the close competitor's profit (assuming it followed suit and reduced its own price). Firm A needs to reduce its costs and strengthen its position against its two main competitors whilst there is scope for growth in the overall market for product X.

Using Figures 4.19 to 4.22 as a basis, various possibilities can be projected for the future, each building on explicit assumptions regarding:

☐ future market demand
☐ likely competitive actions
☐ likely competitive reactions
☐ competitors' liquidity and solvency.

This takes us a long way from conventional single-entity, single-period management accounting, yet the adaptations that need to be made are not so difficult to comprehend – but the benefits from gaining a clearer picture of one's competitive position and how this is changing should be enormous. Strategic management accounting can help realize these benefits.

4.5 SUMMARY

Within this chapter we have been concerned with establishing a base line for *feedforward control*.

As a basis for feedforward control it is necessary to know how resources have been allocated in the past – and with what consequences; this is facilitated by marketing cost analysis. The productivity of marketing activities can be established (both *ex ante* and *ex post*).

Marketing cost analysis can be applied to order-getting and order-filling activities to determine their full costs. When combined with revenue details the net profit from marketing operations will be revealed. Bases of allocation, apportionment and absorption must be chosen carefully if the resulting figures are to be meaningful, but care must also be taken to treat these figures as being indicative rather than definitive. As such, they should be used as a basis for raising questions rather than generating answers.

Marketing segments can be defined in several ways – focusing on channels, customers, territories, products, etc. Once defined, the productivity of each segment can be calculated.

Simmonds offers an alternative approach to establishing a base line by using strategic management accounting to assess competitive position.

<table>
<tr><td>

5

</td><td>

Where next?

</td></tr>
</table>

LEARNING OBJECTIVES

After reading this chapter you should be able to:
- [ ] recognize the relevance of marketing experimentation, the missions approach and marketing programming as means of implementing feedforward control;
- [ ] appreciate the role of standards in a marketing context;
- [ ] evaluate marketing programmes/strategies.

5.1 INTRODUCTION

If the past productivity of a segment (as discussed in Chapter 4) is deemed unsatisfactory, there is scope for varying future inputs (causes) and outputs (effects) via such approaches as marketing experimentation in order to improve future productivity. This is also possible via marketing programming and a missions (or output budgeting) approach.

Within this chapter we will consider a number of ways in which feedforward control can be used in guiding future marketing strategies. It would help to refer back to Figure 3.1 (p. 26) since this chapter addresses the questions raised in Stages Two to Four of that figure.

5.2 SOME APPROACHES

The approaches to be discussed in this section are marketing experimentation, the missions approach and marketing programming.

Marketing experimentation

In a marketing experiment attempts are made to identify the controllable factors that affect a particular dependent variable, and some of these factors are then manipulated systematically in order to isolate and measure their effects on the performance of the dependent variable.

It is not possible, of course, to plan or control all the conditions under which an experiment is conducted: for example, the timing, location and duration of an experiment can be predetermined, but it is necessary to measure such uncontrollable conditions as those caused by the weather and eliminate their effects from the results. Irrespective of these uncontrollable influences, the fact that experiments are concerned with the deliberate manipulation of controllable variables (i.e. such variables as price and advertising effort) means that a good deal more confidence can be placed in conclusions about the effects of such manipulation than if the effects of these changes had been based purely on historical associations.

Studies of marketing costs can provide the ideas for experiments. Questions such as the following can be answered as a result of marketing experimentation:

1. By how much (if anything) would the net profit contribution of the most profitable products be increased if there were an increase in specific marketing outlays, and how would such a change affect the strategy of competitors in terms of the stability of, say, market shares?
2. By how much (if anything) would the net losses of unprofitable products be reduced if there were some decrease in specific marketing outlays?
3. By how much (if anything) would the profit contribution of profitable products be affected by a change in the marketing effort applied to the unprofitable products, and vice versa, and what would be the effect on the total marketing system?
4. By how much (if anything) would the total profit contribution be improved if some marketing effort were diverted to profitable territories or customer groups from unprofitable territorial and customer segments?
5. By how much (if anything) would the net profit contribution be increased if there were a change in the method of distribution to small unprofitable accounts, or if these accounts were eliminated?

Only by actually carrying out properly designed marketing experiments can management realistically predict with an acceptable degree of accuracy the effects of changes in marketing expenditure on the level of sales and profit of each differentiated product, territory or customer segment in the multi-product company.

Experiments must be conducted under conditions that resemble the real-life conditions of the marketplace (in so far as this is possible). It is pointless, for example, carrying out an experiment to prove that the sale of £1's worth of product X in Southampton through medium-sized retailers adds more to profit than does the sale of £1's worth of product Y through small retailers in Newcastle if the market for product X is saturated and no reallocation of marketing resources can change the situation. This points to the danger of confusing what is happening now with what might happen in the future: ascertaining that product X is more profitable than product Y may be the right answer to the wrong question.

The correct style of question should be: 'What will happen to the dependent variable in the future if the independent variables are manipulated now in the following way?' If the concern is with the allocation of sales effort, the aim of an experiment may be to show how changes in the total costs of each sales team can be related to changes in the level of sales revenue. In such a simple case in which only one type of marketing effort is being considered, this effort should be reallocated to those sales segments where an additional unit of effort will yield the highest contribution to net profits.

The experiment can be designed to show which sales segment produces the highest value when the following equation is applied to each in turn:

$$\frac{\text{Additional sales} - \text{Additional variable costs}}{\text{Additional expenditure}}$$

If an additional budget allocation of £1,000 to the London sales force results in extra sales of £5,000 with additional variable costs amounting to £2,000, then the index of performance is

$$\frac{5,000 - 2,000}{1,000} = 3$$

It may happen that the same index computed for the Midlands sales force of the same company has a value of 4, in which case selling effort should be reallocated to the Midlands provided due consideration has been given to the expected level of future demand.

As a result of the high costs involved, experiments must usually be conducted with small samples of the relevant elements. This is generally valid so long as the samples are properly determined and representative. However, it is believed by some that marketing experimentation is not a feasible means by which information can be obtained as a basis for making important decisions.

There are certainly a lot of difficulties to be overcome in planning and executing experiments, and the need to keep special records and make repeated measurements is both expensive and time-consuming. The risk is always present that the results of an experiment will not be of any value because they may not be statistically significant. A further risk is that even temporary and limited experimental variations in the marketing mix may damage sales and customer relationships both during and after the experiment.

Other problems that are involved in marketing experimentation include:

1. the measuring of short-term response when long-term response may be of greater relevance;
2. accurate measurements are difficult to obtain – apart from the high expense involved;
3. it is almost impossible to prevent some contamination of control units by test units since it is difficult to direct variations in the marketing mix solely to individual segments;
4. making experiments sufficiently realistic to be useful is hindered by such difficulties as the national media being less flexible than may be desired, and the fact that competitors may not react to local experimental action in the same way as they would to a national change in policy.

These problems and difficulties, while discouraging, are insufficient to discount completely the use of experimentation as a valuable means of obtaining information to increase the efficiency of marketing operations. Indeed, it is likely that the use of experimental techniques will become increasingly widespread, as has been the case with test marketing which is the best-known form of experimentation in marketing.

The missions approach

In an attempt to develop the relatively simple (hence somewhat deficient) approach to segmental analysis (see Chapter 4) in a way that captures some of the flavour of the complexity of marketing processes the missions approach has been suggested.

A 'mission' in the present context may be defined as the provision of a product or range of products at a particular level of service to a particular customer or customer group in a particular area. Figure 5.1 illustrates three possible marketing missions.

If we take the analysed cost and revenue flows suggested in Figure 5.2 (in what has been termed a 'modularized database approach'), we have a basis for determining the costs, revenues and profits attributable to each mission.

The next step is to superimpose the (horizontal) missions over the (vertical) functional flows in order to produce a missions matrix (as shown in Figure 5.3).

This matrix focuses attention on the purposes to be served (as shown by the missions) and the cost and revenue (hence profit) consequences of carrying out each mission. Within this framework it is possible to consider trade-offs between one course of action and another in a way that was outlined in Chapter 4 on segmental analysis and earlier in this chapter on marketing experimentation. For example, what might be the impact on mission B's performance of an increase in direct sales effort and a decrease in promotional expenditure? Because each mission is multi-dimensional (see Figure 4.1) the risk of information loss is much less than the two-dimensional case shown in Figure 4.17 above.

In effect, reports derived from a missions approach will give information that cuts *across* segments rather than giving it *by* segments.

Marketing programming

Programming is a form of analytical modelling which is useful when it is desired to allocate funds (or other resources) in the best way. The most widely used technique is that of linear programming which aims to determine the optimum allocation of effort

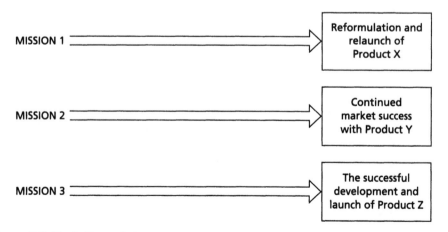

Figure 5.1 Marketing missions

in a situation involving many interacting variables: in other words, it produces the solution that maximizes or minimizes a particular outcome in accordance with given constraints. (For example, how should sales effort be allocated amongst regions to maximize the level of sales subject to a maximum availability of 10,000 units of

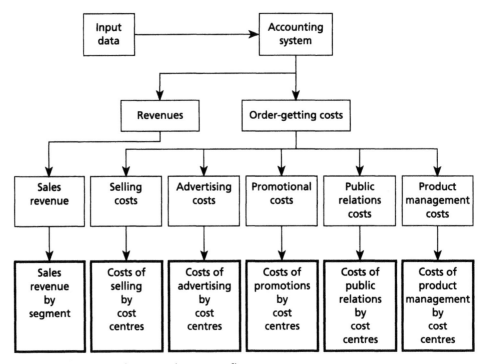

Figure 5.2 Functional cost and revenue flows

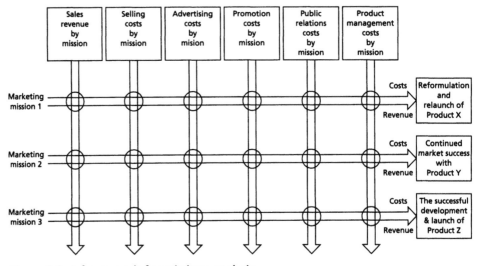

Figure 5.3 A framework for missions analysis

product per period? Or which product mix should be sold – subject to demand – in order to achieve the maximum level of profit?)

In carrying out his or her duties the marketing manager will be interested in making the best use of his or her limited resources, and the constraints that exist will set the upper limit to the level of performance that is possible. For example, the company cannot spend more on advertising than the amount that it has in its advertising appropriation, thus

$$a_1(W) + a_2(X) + a_3(Y) + a_4(Z) \leqslant A$$

where

> $\leqslant$ means 'is equal to or less than'
> A is the total advertising appropriation
> $a_1(W)$ is the amount spent on advertising product W
> $a_2(X)$ is the amount spent on advertising product X
> $a_3(Y)$ is the amount spent on advertising product Y
> $a_4(Z)$ is the amount spent on advertising product Z.

Similarly, a constraint exists in relation to every fixed budget or limited resource such as sales force time or warehouse space:

$$b_1(W) + b_2(X) + b_3(Y) + b_4(Z) \leqslant B$$

where

> B is the total available sales force time
> $b_1(W)$ is the time devoted to selling product W, etc.

and

$$c_1(W) + c_2(X) + c_3(Y) + c_4(Z) \leqslant C$$

where

> C equals the available warehouse space
> $c_1(W)$ is the space occupied by the inventory of W, etc.

The basis on which resources should be allocated is the *marginal response*. If the expenditure on advertising of, say, £100,000 results in sales amounting to £500,000, then the average response is 5/1, and if an increase in advertising expenditure of £1,000 produces additional sales totalling £10,000, this gives the measure of marginal response which is equal to 10/1. Marginal response can thus be seen to be a measure of the value of available opportunities.

If a company's advertising budget is set at £100,000 for a period, the optimal allocation to each of the company's three products (A, B and C) is given by equating the marginal responses because this gives the situation where it will not be beneficial to reallocate funds from one product to another. The requirement, therefore, is to find the best solution to the equation

$$a_1(A) + a_2(B) + a_3(C) = £100,000$$

where

a_1(A) is the advertising budget for product A
a_2(B) is the advertising budget for product B
a_3(C) is the advertising budget for product C.

The solution is given when $\dfrac{\Delta s_1}{\Delta a_1} = \dfrac{\Delta s_2}{\Delta a_2} = \dfrac{\Delta s_3}{\Delta a_3}$

where s_1, s_2, s_3 are the sales of products A, B and C; and

$\dfrac{\Delta s_1}{\Delta a_1}$ is the marginal response for product A

measured as $\dfrac{\text{change in sales}}{\text{change in advertising outlay}}$

and so on for products B and C.

Linear programming must be applied in the absence of uncertainty, which means that uncertainty must be evaluated and eliminated before variables are quantified and put into a linear programming format. Moreover, all the relationships within problems that are to be solved by means of linear programming are assumed to be linear, and this may not apply under all conditions. For example, costs rarely rise in direct proportion to increases in sales volume. But even with this disadvantage, linear programming is still able to indicate the best direction for allocating resources to segments.

5.3 STANDARDS

The ultimate test of efficiency is the relationship of net profit to capital invested, rather than such measures as the ratio of gross profit to sales revenue.

Standard ROI targets can be set to form the foundations for managerial planning, policy-making and special decision-making. Furthermore, ROI permits both internal and external comparisons which lead to the best employment of capital (see Figure 5.4).

However, problems arise over the definition of both the measure of profit and the measure of the investment base. Figure 5.4 shows the ROI calculation, from which the basic equation relating profit to the investment can be extracted:

$$\frac{\text{Sales revenue}}{\text{Capital employed}} \times \frac{\text{Profit}}{\text{Sales revenue}} = \frac{\text{Profit}}{\text{Capital employed}}$$

Capital turnover × Margin on sales = ROI

It is clear from these relationships that, other things being equal, an increase in sales revenue, a reduction in capital employed or a reduction in costs will all result in

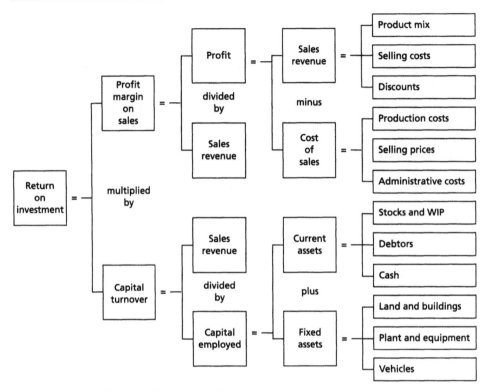

Figure 5.4 Constituents of return on investment

an improved ROI. Management is at times so preoccupied with cost reduction and control that it ignores the need to keep the capital employed down to the minimum level that is consistent with effective performance, or increasing sales revenue from a given capital base.

Whether one is focusing on the setting of ROI targets, or the establishing of less broad standards, this task can be seen as part of the larger problem of motivating individuals towards goal-striving behaviour. The standards and plans are not the goals – they are the agreed means by which the goals may be achieved. The ideal situation is that in which a control system is so designed that it leads people to take actions that are not only in their own self-interests, but also in the interests of the company.

This process is facilitated by considering the *aspiration levels* of the firm's decision makers. The relationship between motivation and levels of aspiration is fairly clear, and revolves around past success/failures and future hopes. Sufficient flexibility should, therefore, be built into the setting of standards to improve motivation by either upwards or downwards movements of targets in order to achieve continuous improvements in performance.

For example, a manager may fail to reach the established plan for reasons beyond his or her control. As a result, the level of aspiration will tend to fall, and motivation will drop accordingly. If this process is to be reversed, a new standard should be set that is attainable (while maintaining an efficient level of performance). If this is done realistically, it should improve the manager's motivation by equating a reasonable standard with the aspiration level.

In essence, the standard should specify what the performance should be under prevailing conditions. For deriving company-wide ROI standards, the emphasis should be on external parameters, taking account of:

1. the achieved ROI of successful competitors in the same industry;
2. the ROI of other leading companies, operating under similar risk and skill circumstances;
3. the position of the company in its own industry, bearing in mind the degree of competitiveness;
4. the level of risk faced, with higher risk usually requiring a higher ROI from the investor's point of view; and
5. the 'expected' ROI – as seen by such groups as trade unions, the financial establishment, creditors.

In connection with more detailed standards of performance, the bases should emphasize internal parameters. If this is not so, the standards will not reflect the firm's particular operating circumstances.

Past performance may be thought a useful basis for determining operating standards, but the danger is that it includes inefficiencies that should not be perpetuated. Current conditions and future expectations are of great relevance, since an attainable level of efficiency can be incorporated into the standards as these conditions dictate.

Attainability is an important dimension of any realistic standard. If standards do not reflect both current and efficient levels of performance, as well as individual aspiration levels, they are not likely to be attainable or to motivate.

The 'ideal' standard of the industrial engineer is not a reasonably attainable level of performance, as it describes a perfect situation. Real-life business conditions are anything but perfect, requiring that the ideal give way to built-in flexibility to accommodate varying circumstances.

In summary, detailed standards should be competitively derived, currently attainable, flexible and agreed with those who are to be held responsible for their attainment.

Marketing standards can be derived to cover such items as:

1. cost to create £1.00 of sales revenue;
2. cost per customer serviced;
3. cost per sales transaction;
4. cost to create £1 of gross contribution;
5. average selling cost of each unit sold;
6. selling prices;
7. discount structures;
8. sales mix;
9. gross sales per salesperson;
10. selling expenses per salesperson;
11. contribution per salesperson;
12. contribution per sales region;
13. contribution per channel of distribution;

14. contribution per order;
15. sales administration costs.

Performance in relation to sales cost standards can reveal that too much sales effort is being devoted to small-account customers, and so on. Studies can be made of sales territories and their potential in order to set standards in the form of sales quotas, time per call, and call frequency. Control of the sales force through standards should provide means of determining and influencing performance to ensure that the target profit contribution is attained.

Let us consider a simple example of standards for sales-force control. The essential control data for monitoring sales-force profitability for Abacus Associates is:

(a) Average total cost of each salesperson	£50,000 p.a.
(b) Average number of calls	1,000 p.a.
(c) Average cost per call ((a) $\div$ (b))	£50
(d) Order:call ratio	1:10
(e) Average cost per order ((c) $\times$ (d))	£500
(f) Average order size (total sales/orders)	£5,000
(g) Product-mix percentage gross contribution	25%
(h) Average profit contribution per order ((f) $\times$ (g))	£1,250
(i) Average number of orders ((b) $\div$ (d))	100
(j) Average profit contribution per salesperson ((h) $\times$ (i))	£125,000

If the average contribution per salesperson (see (j) above) is unsatisfactory, attention can be directed towards the constituent elements (such as order:call ratio and average order size) to see if these can be improved.

The figure given in (a) above for the average total cost of a salesperson can be readily broken down into its fixed and variable components. For example, typical fixed costs are:

☐ salaries;
☐ depreciation on cars;
☐ fixed car expenses (road tax, insurance);
☐ superannuation and other payroll expenses.

On the other hand, variable sales-force costs include:

☐ commissions;
☐ travelling expenses (including car running costs);
☐ entertaining.

Sales quotas can be classified into two categories: those that reflect a desired level of performance, which may not be achieved, although it acts as a strong motivator; and those that are geared to actual expectations. Management must be quite clear which philosophy it wishes to adopt before standards/sales quotas are drawn up.

In general, in order to establish any cost standard, one needs to identify the activity for which a standard is sought and then to measure the inputs to that activity at some acceptable efficiency level.

5.4 EVALUATING MARKET STRATEGIES

In choosing between alternative courses of action or strategies it is, of course, desirable to choose the best; but how is the 'best' to be recognized? The best from the viewpoint of one stakeholder may not be the best from another stakeholder's viewpoint. Similarly, what is best in the short term may not be best in the long term. Specifying the criteria by which choices are to be made between competing alternatives is a crucial step in working towards improved marketing performance.

It has traditionally been the case that financial criteria have dominated choice processes irrespective of the initial emphasis that may have been given to non-financial criteria. Recent changes in strategic thinking have suggested that the dominance of financial measures may no longer be appropriate. For instance, the emphasis placed by McDonald's on quality, service, cleanliness and value shows that a financial criterion is insufficient, although there will invariably be one or more financial measures within any enterprise's set of critical success factors. A selection of the most important financial and non-financial criteria is given in Figure 5.5.

Within the marketing literature there is surprisingly little coverage of effectiveness (i.e. doing the right things) as opposed to efficiency (i.e. doing things right). However, it is implicit in the extensive coverage of efficiency that the results of marketing activities are effective: it is not suggested that effectiveness should be traded off for greater efficiency. Nevertheless, the preoccupation that has existed with inputs rather than outputs tends to mean that outputs such as increased sales revenue, greater market share or higher profits are taken as being self-evident measures of effectiveness. The various inputs and outputs cited in the literature on marketing efficiency include those shown in Figure 5.6.

If we consider market share to be an appropriate output measure we can relate this to the discussion of the PIMS approach (see Chapter 7, pp. 103–6 below). Market share as an output measure features prominently in the PIMS approach (see Abell and Hammond 1979; Buzzell and Gale 1987; Day 1990). ROI is the dependent variable in the PIMS approach with market share playing a key role in the following sequence (which is illustrated in Figure 5.7):

Financial	Non-financial
Liquidity	Sales volume
Cash generation	Market share
Value-added	Growth rate
Earnings per share	Competitive position
Shareholder value	Consumer franchise
Share price	Risk exposure
Profit	Reliance on new products
Profitability	Customer satisfaction
Cost leadership	Sustainable competitive advantage

Figure 5.5 Financial and non-financial criteria

1. superior relative quality is established by a business for its products;
2. this superiority facilitates the building of market share;
3. greater share brings with it cost advantages due to higher volume and experience curve effects;
4. superior quality allows premium prices to be charged, which, in association with lower costs, ensures higher profits and hence enhanced ROI.

Whatever measures of input and output are used in an attempt to assess efficiency – and Figure 5.6 offers only a limited number of each – the overriding emphasis is typically on readily quantifiable factors. This gives a means of both asking and answering the question as to whether the enterprise is getting as much output per unit of input as it should, or whether the efficiency of marketing activities might be improved. As we have seen, however, this concern with 'doing things right' begs the question of whether the right things are being done, which requires a fuller consideration of marketing effectiveness.

Inputs		Outputs
Marketing expense Investment Number and quality of employees Quality of decisions Technology Administrative support	Marketing activities	Profit Sales value Sales volume Market share Cash flow Value-added Consumer franchise

Figure 5.6 Marketing efficiency criteria

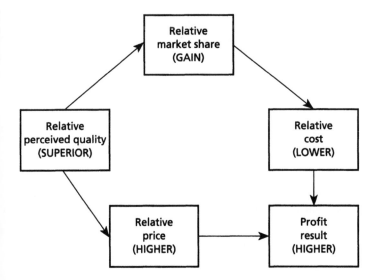

Figure 5.7 Some PIMS linkages

Valuing market strategies

The criterion of enhanced shareholder value has been adopted by Day and Fahey (1988) in their approach to strategy evaluation. Since the basic premise of this approach is that shareholders' interests should be maximized it will be apparent that it is a partial approach that ignores other stakeholders' interests. Moreover, since maximizing the current market value of shareholders' interests presumes that the shares themselves are listed, this restricts Day and Fahey's approach to only some 2,500 of the total of more than 1,000,000 limited companies incorporated within the UK.

Value is created whenever the financial gains from a strategy exceed its costs. The use of discounting methods allows for both the timing of cash flows and the inherent riskiness of marketing strategies in measuring the value of the latter. A potential shareholder will only invest in an enterprise if it is his or her expectation that the management of that enterprise will generate a better return than he or she could obtain himself or herself, at a given level of risk. The minimum expected return is the cost of capital (i.e. that rate used in discounting); hence shareholder value is only created when activities are undertaken that generate a return in excess of the cost of capital.

The usual approach adopted in assessing the shareholder value of an enterprise is to discount the anticipated cash flows by the risk-adjusted cost of capital. If a new strategy is in prospect then the shareholder value will be the sum of the value to be derived from the new strategy plus the 'base-line' value reflecting the value that is expected to result from continuing the existing strategy. This gives a basis for comparing strategic alternatives in a way that highlights their respective contributions to value. Thus:

| Estimated shareholder value if strategy X is selected | = | Estimated value contributed by strategy X | + | Base-line shareholder value. |

Therefore:

| Estimated value of strategy X | = | Estimated shareholder value if strategy X is selected | − | Base-line shareholder value. |

When several competing strategies are being evaluated in a situation in which there are insufficient resources to undertake all available strategies that meet the specified economic criterion (e.g. offer a positive net present value when discounted at the risk-adjusted cost of capital), the recommended basis for ranking acceptable strategies is by use of the present value (PV) index. This shows how much value is created per £1 of investment.

$$\text{PV index} = \frac{\text{Present value of strategy}}{\text{Investment required}}$$

In using this approach to evaluating strategies there needs to be available:

1. cash inflow and outflow forecasts relating to each alternative strategy;
2. cash flow forecasts relating to the base-line strategy;

3. a suitable discount factor (i.e. the risk-adjusted cost of capital);
4. alternative scenarios to allow the sensitivity of the outcomes to changes in the inputs to be tested.

Even if all these information requirements can be met there is inevitably a large element of subjectivity involved: in part this will be included within the estimates of cash flows, etc., and in part it will reflect both the specification of the strategy and the interpretation of results from the analysis. It is suggested that all assumptions involving judgements be specified explicitly in order that their appropriateness can be gauged by others.

The steps to follow in carrying out a strategic evaluation to enhance shareholder value are:

1. derive cash flow forecasts from the managerial judgements relating to competitive and market responses to each strategic alternative;
2. adjust the forecasts from step 1 for risk and timing prior to calculating the net present value (NPV) of each strategy and relating these NPVs to base-line expectations in order to gauge the increase in shareholder value from each alternative;
3. select the strategy that offers the greatest increase in shareholder value and implement it.

It is implicit in this sequence of steps that:

☐ the value creation potential of each strategic alternative relative to the base-line strategy can be accurately predicted;
☐ the shareholder value criterion is applicable to all strategic alternatives having cash-flow implications;
☐ the stock market will recognize and reward strategies that enhance shareholder value.

Each of these matters raises fundamental questions. For example, our ability to predict accurately is limited for reasons of uncertainty as well as personal bias, and the stock market is not a perfect market (and so does not have perfect information on which to base its reactions). Nevertheless, by focusing on cash flows rather than accounting data, and by taking a long-term perspective rather than a short-term one, the approach advocated by Day and Fahey has distinct benefits as well as limitations.

Support for variations on this 'economic value' approach has come from a range of sources. Buzzell and Chussil (1985), for example, have argued that it is rare for managers to evaluate strategies in terms of their effects on future value. This suggests that many enterprises are failing to achieve their full potential by using inappropriate methods for strategic evaluation and by emphasizing short-run financial results at the expense of long-term competitive strength.

5.5 SUMMARY

In this chapter we have dealt with some of the ways in which the financial controller might help in formulating and evaluating future marketing plans.

The analysis suggested in Chapter 4 provides a base-line for improvement, and approaches such as marketing experimentation, output budgeting (or the missions approach) and marketing programming can then be used to identify plans that should lead to enhanced performance.

Standards can be set for a wide range of marketing activities to reflect an efficient level of performance. It is possible to highlight the interdependencies between activities by developing standards within the framework of a ratio pyramid with ROI at the apex. PIMS supplements this approach.

In evaluating alternative marketing programmes/strategies it is desirable to consider both financial and non-financial criteria. Whilst the former may be more readily measured they are not necessarily the more important.

Part 3

Feedback Control

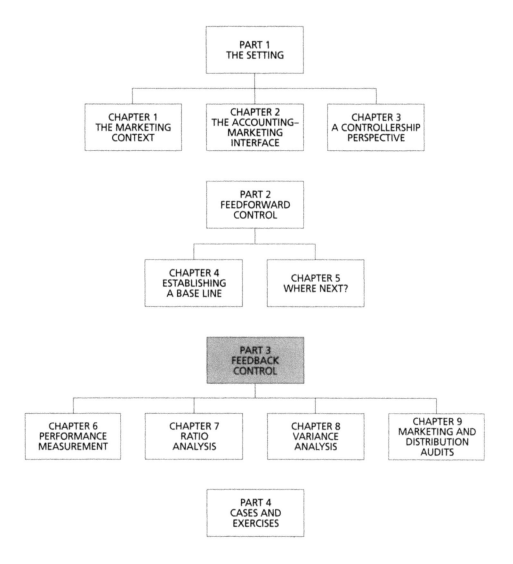

Performance measurement 6

LEARNING OBJECTIVES

After reading this chapter you should be able to:
- ☐ understand the need for performance measurement as a basis for feedback control;
- ☐ recognize the importance of personalizing responsibility if control is to be effective;
- ☐ apply the principle of management by exception;
- ☐ perceive the need to have a broader approach to performance measurement than that of profitability analysis;
- ☐ appreciate some of the behavioural problems in marketing control – such as bias and entrapment.

6.1 INTRODUCTION

Performance measurement is concerned with assessing the efficiency of converting inputs into outputs and the effectiveness of the actual outputs. This can be considered from two points of view:

- ☐ the firm as a whole; and
- ☐ the sub-systems of the firm.

Factors to consider are what was achieved, how well it was achieved and the profit or cost of the achievement. Although both quantitative and qualitative measures of success exist, the present concern is with the former, based on the setting of some standard of desired performance for purposes of comparison with the actual level of performance.

In measuring output it must be realized that performance measurement has more than one dimension. Consequently, in relation to inputs and the efficiency of their conversion into outputs, it is appropriate to ask:

- ☐ How much was achieved?
- ☐ How good was this achievement?
- ☐ How much did it cost?

It is perhaps paradoxical that performance can only be appraised after the event, as this means that nothing can be done to change what has happened or, in most instances, what is currently happening.

Nonetheless, we have seen that control involves guiding current and future operations in the light of the experience of the past, in accordance with a plan. The plan enables the individual to know in advance what is expected and how it will be assessed. As a result, every attempt should be made to achieve the plan.

The reaction of individuals to control will vary, depending upon:

☐ the type of individuals and tasks involved;
☐ the environment in which operations are conducted;
☐ the means and timing of the control effort.

However, feedback control only takes place after actual results have deviated from planned results; hence the effectiveness of control hinges critically upon the setting of plans and standards that are to be achieved, as well as the follow-up response.

Marketing managers tend to view their success or failure in terms that are different from the criteria that are characteristic of accountants' reports. As mentioned earlier, the introspective concern with cost data and transactions on the part of the accountant is in marked contrast to the marketer's interest in competitive position (as indicated by relative market share, potential for market growth and product life-cycle patterns).

From the point of view of cost control, given a particular organization structure, individual categories of marketing expenditure can be divided into fixed and variable types, their behaviour patterns can be established, and standards can be set via budgets or standard costs. It is therefore possible for comparisons to be made between actual outlays and desired (or standard) outlays as in any other area of cost control. A general understanding of cost behaviour, cost–volume–profit relationships and relevant costing is a fundamental prerequisite to the control of any category of cost. Within the marketing sphere, however, the influence of external factors is more strongly felt, and this raises measurement problems relating both to the prediction of outcomes in the face of very many internal–external interactions and to the identifying of causal relationships when attempting to evaluate, for instance, the effectiveness of advertising outlays. The key to controlling marketing activities lies in the very careful planning of marketing activities, provided that plans are flexible and drawn up in accordance with the principles of contingency planning. (For example, if it is expected that product X will secure a 10 per cent share of its market segment which, in total, is expected to amount to sales of 100,000 units during the next period, a detailed plan should be compiled that not only gives consideration to this size and share but also considers 'what if . . .?' questions. What if the market demand is 75,000 units, or 125,000 units? What if our share with product X is 12 per cent or 8 per cent?)

Cost control must look at both the actual and the desired patterns of expenditure and the effectiveness (which is equivalent to quality) of the expenditure, and this is far from being an easy task. To what extent, for example, is a given level of sales due to the ability or personality of the salesperson, the characteristics of the customer, features of the product itself, competitive offerings, general business conditions, or the effect of advertisements and other promotional activity?

6.2 RESPONSIBILITY ACCOUNTING

Responsibility accounting is the approach whereby costs, revenues, etc., are planned and accumulated in accordance with organizational responsibilities, and communicated to and from the individuals responsible for their incurrence.

The need for responsibility accounting follows from certain well-established principles of control. To be held responsible for any results, the individual manager should:

(a) know what he or she is expected to achieve;
(b) know from time to time what he or she is actually achieving;
(c) have the power to regulate what is happening (i.e. to bring (a) and (b) together).

When all these conditions do not exist simultaneously, it may be unjust and ineffective to hold an individual responsible for the level of costs or profit realized, and the desired control will not be achieved.

From a planning point of view, responsibility accounting is important because, being based on clearly defined areas of responsibility, it enables responsible individuals to play the major role in planning. Regardless of size, planning only makes sense if all levels of management are involved. Thus the managers who are held responsible for performance have a right to participate in setting the goals and levels of performance that they must achieve as part of the overall corporate effort. In this way, human relations should be improved through greater involvement, more job satisfaction, and the avoidance of duplicated effort and hence clashes.

A *responsibility centre* is essentially a personalized concept and represents the sphere of influence of a specific manager. By compiling plans from responsibility centres, and considering results attributable to the controllable costs, revenues and profits at each level of authority, financial control crosses the threshold into behavioural science, especially in the area of motivation.

Once the manager has submitted the plans, it is imperative that he or she be informed of any modification, and the reasoning behind it. If this is not done, the manager may lose confidence in the attainability of the plan (no matter how specific it may be), and fail to see how it fits into the overall corporate pattern. The guiding principle is that those held responsible should be consulted on all matters appertaining to that responsibility.

In summary, the implications of fixing responsibility are as follows:

1. The organizational structure must be clearly defined, and responsibility delegated so that each person knows his or her role.
2. The extent and limits of functional control must be determined.
3. The responsible individuals should be fully involved in preparing plans if they are to be held responsible for results.
4. Responsible individuals must be serviced with regular performance reports.
5. Means must be established to enable plans to be revised in line with actual performance in such a way that responsible individuals are involved.
6. Every item should be the responsibility of some individual within the organization.

The ability to delegate is a sign of a good manager, and responsibility accounting facilitates this. Specifically charging managers with responsibility for a segment of the business is the best-known way of ensuring that they perform satisfactorily.

6.3 MANAGEMENT BY EXCEPTION

Against the background of responsibility accounting what can be suggested to help the management accountant in developing budgets to facilitate performance evaluation and the control of marketing activities?

As a starting point the senior managers of the organization must specify the desired outcomes for both marketing and financial performance. This will include a specification of, *inter alia*:

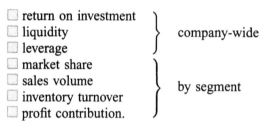

- ☐ return on investment ⎫
- ☐ liquidity   ⎬ company-wide
- ☐ leverage   ⎭
- ☐ market share   ⎫
- ☐ sales volume   ⎪
- ☐ inventory turnover   ⎬ by segment
- ☐ profit contribution. ⎭

Such benchmarks as these facilitate more detailed budgeting, and in this task it is possible to make use of cost standards.

It cannot be expected that standards will be met perfectly, so some measure of the significance of results *via-à-vis* standards must be developed. This involves the setting of tolerance limits, with results falling beyond these limits being the subject of control and investigation, while those falling within the limits are accepted as being satisfactory. The tolerance range should not be so broad as to excuse all levels of performance, nor so narrow as to cause control action to be instigated too frequently.

The basic instrument of control in this respect is the statistical control chart (see Figure 6.1). This allows successive levels of performance for a particular factor to be observed in relation to standards and to tolerance limits. The example given in the figure illustrates the control of advertising expenditure. As a percentage of sales revenue, this is allowed to fluctuate around a standard of 10 per cent, but as soon as it exceeds a tolerance of 2 per cent either way, it is investigated to identify the cause.

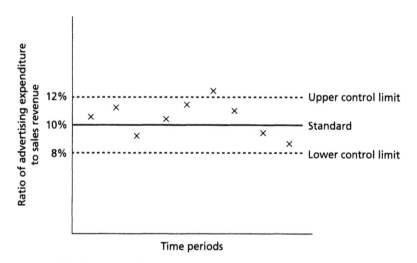

Figure 6.1 Statistical control chart

The reason may be, in this example, the entry into the market of a new competitor, causing an increase in advertising effort on the part of the company to regain lost sales. (The ratio can vary, of course, through either a constant sales level with varying advertising expenditure or constant advertising with changing sales.) A change in prevailing conditions should result in a reassessment of the standard and a modification of the levels of tolerance.

The statistical control chart is based on the well-known statistical principle that significant variances are those that do not arise purely through chance circumstances. Consequently, the tolerance range should be sufficiently wide to accommodate variations from standard that are purely due to chance. The assumption is that results falling beyond the tolerance limits are attributable to identifiable controllable causes and not to chance and are, therefore, worthy of investigation.

This discussion is concerned with the approach known as *management by exception*. A control system operated on this principle is one in which management's attention is drawn to the relatively small number of items having significant variances from plan. Consequently, little attention needs to be paid to the relatively large number of items conforming to plan. This permits managers to focus their attention on planning for the future, instead of becoming submerged in day-to-day trivia. Past events cannot be altered – only their impact on the future can be affected by management action. Management by exception is the means to improving future operations on the basis of knowledge from the past.

6.4 PROFITABILITY ANALYSIS

Profitability can be defined as the rate at which profit is generated. This may be expressed as profit (i.e. an output measure) per unit of input (e.g. investment or some measure of effort such as sales calls). Apart from limiting our focus to one output measure (profit) to represent effectiveness, this approach also overlooks such issues as the quality of services rendered, hence its partiality needs to be kept in mind.

As a criterion for strategic decision-making, profitability has been criticized by Robinson *et al.* (1978), as being insufficient, in:

☐ failing to provide a systematic explanation as to why one business sector has more favourable prospects than another and why one enterprise's position in a particular sector is strong or weak;
☐ not providing enough insight into the underlying dynamics and balance of an enterprise's individual business units and the balance between them.

Other writers (including Chakravarthy (1986) and Day (1990)) have also criticized profitability as a performance criterion because of its remoteness from the actions that actually create value: it represents an outcome rather than a determinant of performance and cannot be managed directly – hence employees are likely to attach limited importance to it on the grounds that their day-to-day actions would appear to have little impact on profitability.

Feder (1965) has defined good marketing performance as existing when investment in each market segment is made to the point where the expenditure of an additional $1 or £1 would produce greater immediate profits if spent elsewhere. This approach reflects the *marginal responsiveness* that is characteristic of marketing experimentation. (i.e. Where can the greatest response in terms of improved profit be achieved for a marginal increase in effort?). To take an example, if investment of £1 million in advertising within a given market produces sales of £20 million and a gross margin of £10 million, then the *average* response of profit to advertising is 10:1. If an increase in advertising expenditure of £100,000 produced additional sales of £3 million and a gross margin of £1.5 million, then the *marginal* response would be 15:1.

In assessing marketing performance using this approach it would be logical to determine the average response for the existing allocation of marketing effort, segment by segment, which would highlight those areas in which the company has underspent or overspent relative to their profit potential. Improvements can be made by allocating additional effort in accordance with the anticipated marginal response: the greater the anticipated marginal response the more efficient will be the allocation of effort. In considering whether additional effort might be exerted through direct selling, advertising, or improved terms for intermediaries within distribution channels, for example, the need exists to consider the timing factor since different actions bring results over different time scales.

A less dynamic approach, emphasizing profit (rather than profitability), has been suggested by a number of writers. Goodman (1970a) and Pyne (1984) both offer modified versions of financial operating statements as bases for assessing marketing performance. These are illustrated in Figures 6.2 and 6.3.

In Figure 6.2 Goodman distinguishes carefully between direct and apportioned costs, which is a more relevant distinction than, say, that between fixed and variable costs if one is concerned to identify the performance of a marketing segment: relevance is given priority over the question of cost behaviour. In principle it makes sense to separate the profit attributable to manufacturing, distribution and so forth, on a direct cost basis. The operational difficulty in doing this stems from the problems associated with identifying the direct costs of product 123 within a product range of 10,000 items.

Apart from the quantity of products as a measure of performance we might also consider the quality of profits. This depends upon the position of a particular product within its life cycle. It is evident that the profits from products in the growth phase of the cycle are likely to be more valuable than those in the decline phase since the former have a more promising future.

Pyne's approach is similar in some respects to that of Goodman. For instance, both authors emphasize the need for conventional operating statements (i.e. those having a legalistic format) to be modified to reflect marketing's circumstances and, in so doing, to highlight direct costs.

In Figure 6.3 we can see that Pyne's approach differs in some significant ways from that of Goodman:

☐ revenue is analysed more fully;
☐ marketing costs are analysed more fully with headings that help in distinguishing operating from policy-related costs;
☐ the orientation is more radical than that of Goodman in giving a basis for assessing marketing performance in strategic terms.

The amount of profit an enterprise earns is a measure of its effectiveness if that enterprise has a profit objective. (In this sense we can define effectiveness in terms of achieving that which one sought to achieve.) Since profit = revenue (output) − cost

	£	£
Proceeds from sales		100.0
Variable cost of goods sold:		
Raw materials	10.0	
Packing	10.0	
Direct labour	5.0	
Variable gross profits (manufacturing contribution margin)		75.0
Other variable expenses:		
Freight	3.0	
Warehousing	2.0	
Spoilage	1.0	
Commissions	5.0	
Discounts	3.0	
Variable profit (distribution contribution margin)		61.0
Direct product costs:		
Advertising	9.0	
Promotion	3.0	
Direct product profits		49.0
Direct division costs:		
Sales management	12.0	
Product management	3.0	
Sales force	2.8	
Sales incentives	1.0	
Market research	0.2	
Division profit contribution (net contribution margin)		30.0
Allocated fixed expense:		
Factory indirect costs	21.0	
Supervision	4.0	
Other indirect costs	19.0	
Corporate administration	5.0	
Net division profit before taxes		(19.0)

Figure 6.2 Marketing-oriented income statement
(Source: adapted from Goodman 1970a: 38)

(input), it can be seen to be a measure of efficiency also in that it relates outputs to inputs. Thus an organization having revenues of £100 million and costs of £60 million is more efficient that one in the same industry having revenues of £100 million and costs of £70 million since the former uses less input to produce a given output.

Despite its ability to act as a measure both of effectiveness and efficiency, profit is a less than perfect measure because:

1. it is a monetary measure, and monetary measures do not measure all aspects of either input or output;

Full revenue sales (at full sale price to end user)	£
Lost revenue	
Distributors' mark-ups and margins	
Mark-downs, offers, deals and allowances	
Third-party costs of delivery to end user paid by the purchaser	
Sales proceeds	£
Sales taxes and customs duties	
Net sales proceeds	£
Direct marketing expenses	
Direct selling – field sales expenses	
Sales promotion – merchandising and display	
– samples, point of sales aids	
– cooperative allowances to distributors	
Product packaging and branding expense	
Product service – installation, warranty and returns	
Warehousing – storage, receiving and marking, shipping	
Transportation outward – truck, rail, air; cost, insurance, freight and delivery	
Direct marketing contribution	£
Managed marketing expenses	
Order processing	
Sales and distribution management	
Brand and product management	
Marketing direction and administration	
Marketing policy costs	£
Advertising and publicity	
Market research and customer relations	
Product planning, design and development	
Marketing team training and development	
Committed marketing costs	£
Inventory carrying – expense and financing	
Cost of credit – collection and financing	
Marketing equipment – maintenance, insurance, financing	
Net marketing contribution	£

Figure 6.3 Marketing-oriented profit statement

Note: where appropriate, lost revenue may be broken down by the marketing channels in use, e.g. wholesalers, stockists, retail chains, stores, direct vending outlets, etc.

(Source: Pyne 1984: 90)

2. the standards against which profits are judged may themselves be less than perfect;
3. at best, profits are a measure of what has happened in the short run whereas we must also be interested in the long-run consequences of management actions.

The most common tendency in commercial enterprises is to focus on the short-run maximization of net profit (or sales) without considering the damage that this might do to the long-run position (e.g. by postponing repairs or maintenance work; by cutting back on advertising or on research, training or quality control expenditure; by deferring capital investment outlays; or through exhortations to employees to increase productivity). Short-term 'gains' achieved in this way tend to be illusory because the subsequent need to make up lost ground (e.g. via heavier advertising or training in later periods) is likely to more than outweighs short-term gains.

Saunders (1987) has observed that an enterprise only has two basic ways of increasing wealth: it can do this by innovating to increase its volume or seeking to improve its productivity by producing the same output but at lower cost. It is much simpler to look inwards and seek to cut costs rather than to look outwards and seek to innovate, compete more effectively or increase margins through better marketing planning. Cost cutting is referred to by many Europeans as 'a British solution' in that it is easy to do in the short term but with unfortunately long-term consequences (as suggested in the previous paragraph). Figure 6.4 summarizes the alternative approaches to improving long-run returns.

As is apparent from Figure 6.4, a preoccupation with short-term profit reflects an introspective concern with aspects of productivity. A longer-term perspective requires a shift of focus from internal productivity improvement to external factors – such as

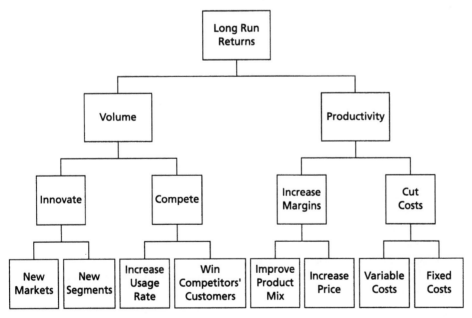

Figure 6.4 Strategic alternatives
(Source: Saunders 1987: 174)

beating the competition and innovating (by developing new markets, new products or both).

In essence what is needed is an approach that avoids a preoccupation with only one factor, but which seeks to balance the factors it considers. A particular approach to balance which has been enthusiastically received in recent years is Kaplan and Norton's *balanced scorecard framework* (1992, 1993) which 'provides executives with a comprehensive framework that translates a company's strategic objectives into a coherent set of performance measures, thereby providing a powerful tool for decision making'.

Within their framework Kaplan and Norton specify four sets of goals and associated performance measures which focus attention on the following basic questions:

- How do customers see us? (i.e. customer perspective)
- At what must we excel? (i.e. internal business perspective)
- Can we continue to improve and create value? (i.e. innovation and learning perspective)
- How do we look to our shareholders? (i.e. financial perspective)

These elements of the scorecard are illustrated in Figure 6.5, from which it will be apparent that this approach has the potential to overcome two of the most pervasive problems associated with, on the one hand, univariate performance measures and, on the other, linking goals and measures of performance.

To implement the balanced scorecard approach it is necessary that senior managers address four further questions regarding:

- their vision of the future;
- the ways in which they will be seen to differ in shareholders' perceptions, customers' perceptions, internal management activities and their ability to innovate and grow if their vision succeeds;
- the specification of critical success factors from financial, customer, internal and innovating perspectives;
- the critical measurements which should be used for each of the four goal and performance areas shown in Figure 6.5.

As Murray and O'Driscoll (1996: 386) point out, the balanced scorecard framework improves on traditional approaches in some significant ways. For example:

1. It is based on the company's strategic objectives and competitive demands; by demanding that managers select a small number of critical indicators it promotes greater focus on strategic vision.
2. By including financial and non-financial measures it provides a basis for managing both current and future success.
3. It balances external and internal goals and measures and reveals trade-offs that managers should or should not make.
4. It facilitates coherence between various strategic initiatives and special projects (such as re-engineering, total quality and empowerment initiatives) by providing a goal-related context and an approach to integrated measurement.

	Goals	Measures
How do we look to our shareholders? *Financial perspective*	• survive • succeed • prosper	• cash flow • sales growth and operating income at division level • ROE, share of market
How do customers see us? *Customer perspective*	• new products • responsiveness • preference • partnership	• new products as % sales • performance delivery • % key account purchases • no. of joint projects
What must we excel at? *Internal business perspective*	• technology ability • operations excellence • R&D productivity • NPD activity	• application turnaround • yield % • fastest output • introduction schedule vs plan
Can we continue to improve and create value? *Innovation and learning perspective*	• technology leadership • process improvement • time to market	• first with next generation • downtime % • cycle time vs industry norm

Figure 6.5 The balanced scorecard
(Source: adapted from Kaplan and Norton 1992: 76)

6.5 SOME BEHAVIOURAL ASPECTS

From a behavioural point of view the impact on a manager's motivation is likely to be adverse when performance investigations are in prospect due to the empirical tendency for investigations to be associated with failure. Machines may be unaffected by the presence of control mechanisms, but human behaviour is inevitably influenced by the prospect of investigation.

Organizational rewards – which include remuneration, promotions, etc. – are the principal means by which top management seeks to motivate subordinates towards effective performance. Via their involvement in measuring performance accountants are associated with the reward process – and this almost certainly plays a role in influencing attitudes towards accountants and their function (see Emmanuel *et al.* 1990).

Irrespective of its technical design, the effectiveness of any managerial accounting system will be influenced by the way in which the information it produces is used. This is particularly important in the context of evaluating individual managers' performance, as in the case of variance reporting.

Success in meeting budget targets is unlikely to be perfect so some conflict is invariably found as a feature of organizational life. To some extent this manifests itself in variances, but it also results in behaviour colloquially termed 'playing the system'. This arises because managers focus their attention on that which is being measured and by which their performance will be judged – irrespective of its organizational relevance. Examples include bias in setting budgets (see Lowe and Shaw 1968; Schiff and Lewin 1970).

In a more recent paper Otley (1985) has suggested that budget estimates are rarely precisely attained for two primary reasons:

1. the forecasting models that managers use are imperfect and give rise to errors;
2. the reward systems under which managers operate may prompt them to bias both the level at which budget estimates are set and the actual performance that is reported.

The second of these reasons accords with points made above about 'playing the system': managers 'deliberately influence the budget-setting process so as to obtain budgets which differ from their best estimates of actual outcomes and they may then adjust their actual behaviour so that some desired relationship between actual and budgeted performance is obtained' (Otley 1985: 415). This illustrates the notion of *organizational slack* which is allocated to different parts of an organization via the budgetary process through the tendency of managers to *understate* expected revenues and to *overstate* expected costs. The underlying logic is that performance will appear favourable if the under-/overstated budget is accepted and actual outcomes are in line with unbiased expected outcomes, or that attainment of the budget will still be feasible even if the manager's superiors tighten up the initial biased estimates.

It should be apparent that the use of creative talent to ensure that the message conveyed by budgetary information (i.e. the elimination of variances due to manipulation of the initial estimates or actual performance) serves the manager's own interests rather than those of the organization, is a waste, and fails to bring about control actions that are conducive to organizational effectiveness.

Entrapment

In dealing with such activities as new product development and launch one is dealing with *projects*. A project can be defined as a set of activities intended to accomplish a specified end result of sufficient importance to be of interest to management.

> In a project, the focus of control is on the project itself, rather than on activities in a given time period in individual responsibility centers, as is the case with the management control of ongoing operations.
>
> (Anthony 1988: 16)

There are three aspects of particular interest within a project:

☐ its scope (i.e. the specifications for the end product);
☐ its schedule (i.e. the time required);
☐ its cost.

Trade-offs between scope, schedule and cost are usually possible in projects. For example, costs might be reduced by decreasing the project's scope, or the schedule might be reduced by increasing the cost. This is not always easy to plan since performance standards are likely to be less reliable for a one-off project than for ongoing activities. Moreover, projects tend to be influenced to a greater extent by the external environment than is the case with continuing operations.

The prospect of being assessed as part of the control endeavour – whether in relation to projects or ongoing activities – typically affects the behaviour of individuals, often with dysfunctional consequences. Control activities are far from neutral in their impact, as can be shown by means of a phenomenon of recent interest:

entrapment. This occurs when a responsible individual increases his or her commitment to an ineffective course of action in order to justify the previous allocation of resources to that task. Entrapment is seen as being one example of a broader psychological process that focuses on commitment. The commitment of an individual to a particular course of action is likely to depend on, *inter alia* (see Brockner *et al.* 1986: 110):

1. responsibility for the action;
2. responsibility for the consequences of the action;
3. the salience of the action;
4. the consequences of the action.

While entrapment is not easily explained in terms of economic rationality, there are various plausible explanations reflecting psychological rationality. For example (after Wilson and Zhang 1997):

☐ there is a need for the decision maker to assert him- or herself and reaffirm the wisdom of his or her initial decision;
☐ the initial commitment was made as a result of the decision maker's belief in the goodness of the course of action, hence self-justification, justification to others, and the norms of consistency are served by continuing;
☐ continuing avoids the waste of the investment already made (which is known as the 'sunk-cost fallacy');
☐ further investment gives further opportunities for the project to come good;
☐ negative feedback is treated as a learning experience (i.e. a cue to revise the inputs rather than cancel the project);
☐ negative feedback, alternatively, may be seen as a chance variation;
☐ a state of inertia has been created by which a project's financial past cannot be divorced from its future – prior investment then motivates the decision to continue;
☐ decisions are not made in a social vacuum, hence social costs and benefits must be considered relating to self-image, organizational image, reputation and face-saving – continue so long as the social and psychological benefits are greater than the economic costs;
☐ information processing has behavioural underpinnings, such as selective perception in which we see what we want to see;
☐ an organization's reward system may work to encourage the decision maker to overlook short-term setbacks and continue with the original project through bad times.

A variation on the theme of entrapment is that of escalation (e.g. see Staw and Ross 1987a, 1987b). These two phenomena are often related but are analytically separable: entrapment may exist in the absence of escalation. Vivid examples of escalation have been experienced in many major projects when the cost out-turns prove to be much greater than anticipated, including the Sydney Opera House, Concorde, the Channel Tunnel.

6.6 SUMMARY

Within this chapter we have looked at some aspects of performance measurement in the context of feedback control. This deals with the final question posed in Figure 3.1: how can we ensure arrival?

The fact that performance measurement (under feedback control) can only be gauged after the event does not invalidate its potential usefulness – although plans are needed to provide benchmarks.

To facilitate feedback control performance measures need to be personalized, which requires the adoption of *responsibility accounting*. Under this approach cost incurrence, revenue generation, profit achievement, etc., are personalized according to whoever can influence the factor in question. Within this setting it is helpful to employ *management by exception* in order that attention might be focused on performance measures that are significantly wide of their mark.

Profitability analysis was discussed but care needs to be taken to avoid emphasizing this (or any other single factor) at the expense of other critical aspects of performance. The balanced scorecard deliberately seeks to embrace a range of criteria to avoid too narrow a focus.

Finally, some behavioural issues were considered, such as bias in the budgeting process and entrapment within the management of projects, which can cause problems in controlling marketing activities.

Ratio analysis 7

LEARNING OBJECTIVES

After reading this chapter you should be able to:
- ☐ appreciate the role of ratio analysis in securing control over marketing activities;
- ☐ develop an appropriate set of ratios;
- ☐ recognize the potential of the PIMS database.

7.1 INTRODUCTION

Whether one's primary interest is in the productivity of an organization as a whole, or in the productivity of a highly specific activity within an organization, ratios can be computed at a suitable level of aggregation. Their value lies in the relative measures (as opposed to absolute measures) on which they are based.

It is possible to calculate a great range of ratios, but a word of warning is needed to ensure that only useful ratios are calculated. Thus, for example, the ratio of

$$\frac{\text{Advertising expenditure}}{\text{Miles travelled by salespersons}}$$

within a given period is not likely to be very useful for at least two reasons:

1. it seeks to relate two input factors (rather than one input and one output);
2. the resulting ratio (of advertising expenditure per mile travelled by salespersons) is not meaningful.

On the other hand, the ratio of

$$\frac{\text{Incremental sales revenue}}{\text{Incremental promotion}}$$

relates one input to a relevant output and is potentially useful as a measure of promotional effectiveness. Discretion, therefore, is most important in choosing which ratios to calculate as a means towards assessing productivity within marketing.

Another warning needs to be given over the way in which ratios tend to average out any patterns in the underlying data. Consider the case of a seasonal business making 90 per cent of its sales in the first six months of every year and the remaining 10 per cent during the other six months. Average monthly sales over the whole year will differ significantly from the average monthly sales in each half-year, so one must choose carefully the period over which one gathers data and the frequency with which one calculates ratios.

7.2 DEVELOPING RATIOS

At an organizational level the ultimate measure of short-term efficiency is the relationship between net profit and capital employed, typically expressed in percentage terms as the rate of return on capital employed or the rate of return on investment (ROI).

$$\frac{\text{Net profit}}{\text{Capital employed}} \times 100 = \text{ROI.}$$

This ratio shows the return (i.e. net output) that has been generated by the capital employed (i.e. input) during a given period of time. Problems exist in connection with the definitions, and hence measurement, of both numerator and denominator, which highlights another note of caution in using ratios: always be sure to establish the definition of numerators and denominators. For example, is the net profit pre-tax or post-tax? Is the capital employed based on historic cost or replacement cost figures?

Given that profit is the residual once costs have been deducted from revenues, it is clear that ROI can be improved by increasing revenues, decreasing costs or reducing capital employed – or by any combination of these. This gives us the basic idea underlying the ratio pyramid. At the apex is the primary ratio (ROI), but this can be decomposed into two secondary ratios (as shown in Figure 5.4 on p.73):

$$\text{Primary ratio:} \quad \frac{\text{net profit}}{\text{capital employed}}$$

$$\text{Secondary ratios:} \quad \frac{\text{net profit}}{\text{sales revenue}}, \frac{\text{sales revenue}}{\text{capital employed}}$$

Each of the secondary ratios can help explain the ROI. The first is the profit rate (or margin) on sales and the second is the capital turnover. Their interrelationship is such that:

Profit rate $\times$ Capital turnover = ROI

The general cause of any deviation in ROI from standard may be found by computing the profit ratio and the capital turnover ratio, but this is only a starting point. Even the secondary ratios are highly aggregated, so it may be necessary to proceed to measure further ratios as one moves down the ratio pyramid using its structure as a diagnostic guide. Before corrective action can be taken a study of specific causes must be made, hence *tertiary ratios* need to be worked out.

Tertiary ratios are those that constitute the secondary ratios. The profit ratio reflects the relationship between the gross profit rate, the level of sales and operating costs (i.e. net profit + operating costs = gross profit), while the rate of capital turnover is affected by the level of sales and the capital structure mix (of fixed and working capital, etc.). From these details it is a simple step to compute four tertiary ratios as follows:

1. $\dfrac{\text{Gross profit}}{\text{Sales revenue}}$

2. $\dfrac{\text{Sales revenue}}{\text{Operating costs}}$

3. $\dfrac{\text{Sales revenue}}{\text{Fixed assets}}$

4. $\dfrac{\text{Sales revenue}}{\text{Working capital}}$

Many other levels of the ratio pyramid can be identified, and the process of decomposing broad ratios into their component parts can be continued further and further until the reasons for variances are known. If, for example, the tertiary ratio of sales revenue to working capital (i.e. ratio 4 above) was broken down further, it will be seen to be made up of two ratios, which themselves are made up of many more subordinate ratios, as in Figure 7.1.

The decomposition can still go on because, for instance, the ratio of sales to stock is made up as shown in Figure 7.2.

An overall ratio pyramid is given in Figure 7.3 and part of this (relating to marketing) is developed and examined in greater detail in Figure 7.4.

Figure 7.5 illustrates a ratio pyramid developed specifically for distribution activities.

The focus on ROI prompts the question – to what extent is marketing expenditure in the nature of capital investment rather than revenue expense? This is a grey area.

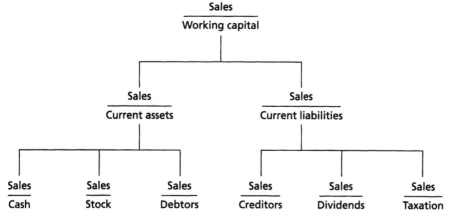

Figure 7.1 Sales to working capital ratio

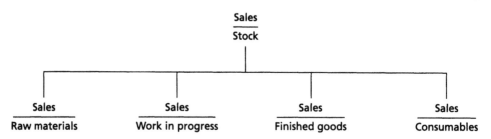

Figure 7.2 Sales to stock ratio

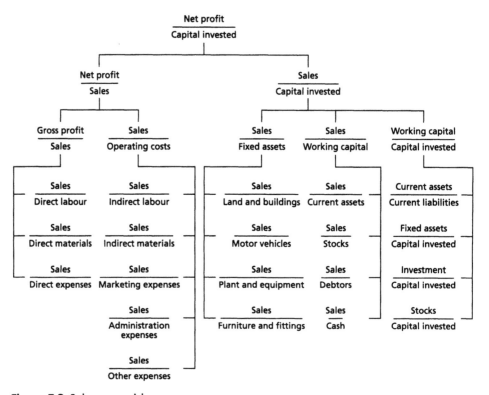

Figure 7.3 Sales pyramid

In the case of investment in manufacturing capacity, by contrast, there is widespread agreement on the range of items to be included in the investment base but, in building marketing capacity (e.g. via research studies, product development, promotional activities and training programmes), there is a tendency to treat costs as being current (to be charged immediately against revenue) rather than capital outlays (which have earning potential over a longer period), thereby suggesting that markets have no value. (The obvious exception, arising in take-over situations, is goodwill, which represents the capital value of an enterprise over and above the value of its physical and net financial resources. But, as a realistic measure of marketing investment, it is unhelpful – not least of all because it is measured by accountants'

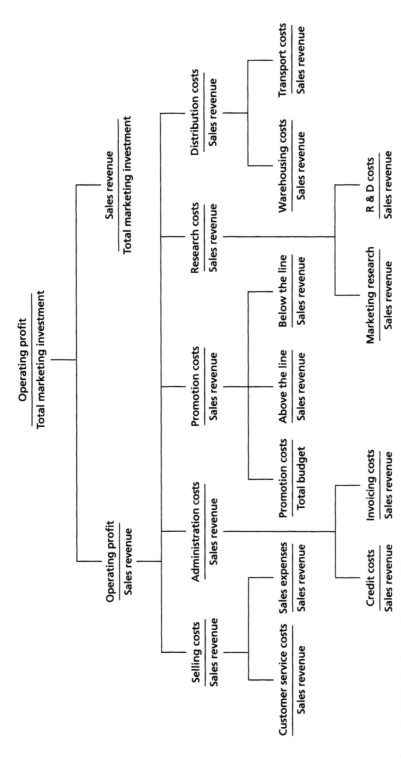

Figure 7.4 Marketing ratio pyramid

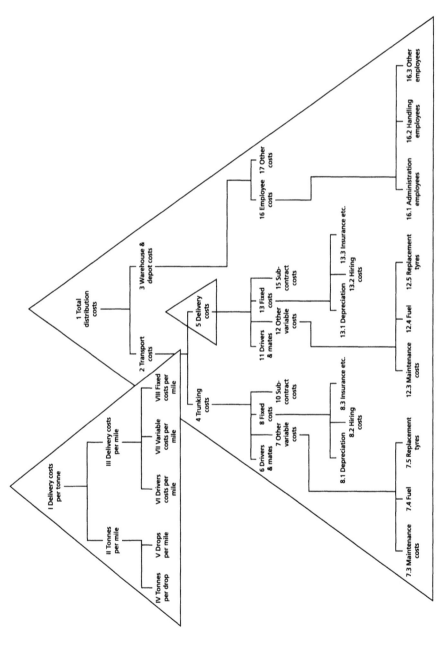

Figure 7.5 Distribution ratio pyramid

simplistic formulae rather than by focusing on the underlying marketing determinants.)

However, it is primarily through its marketing investment that an enterprise is able to justify investment in production and distribution facilities, and so the question of defining marketing investment is worthy of attention in order to help managers evaluate resource allocation choices *ex ante* and to give a reference point for measuring performance *ex post*. (In particular, marketing investment is the independent variable on which sales volume depends, whereas manufacturing investment is dependent upon sales volume, so a clearer understanding is most desirable.)

Any investment base must be linked to a measure of profit if performance (in terms of a rate of return on investment) is to be assessed. Managers in general are *au fait* with this approach for organizations as a whole, but work is needed in relating appropriate measures of marketing investment and marketing profit to determine marketing profitability. This may be done for marketing activities *in toto*, or for particular elements (e.g. sales operations, channel activities, product lines). For each, it should be possible to define the attributable investment base (including, say, stocks, debtors, cars, training, consumer research and promotions in the case of a sales region), and to relate to this a measure of marketing profit for that element.

If the measure of performance for an element is given by

$$\frac{\text{Profit}}{\text{Investment}} \times 100$$

it follows that this can be improved (i.e. productivity can be increased) by either increasing profit or reducing investment. The major difficulty lies in linking specific outcomes (profit) to specific inputs (the investment), especially over long future periods.

If resource allocation (and subsequent utilization) in marketing (and hence its contribution to society as a whole) is to be improved, the aim must be to direct marketing effort (investment) into marketing activities (sales areas, advertising campaigns, etc.) to the point where further effort would yield no additional benefit (i.e. where the resources would be better employed elsewhere). The difficulty again is one of relating investment to profit as one develops and executes marketing strategies.

7.3 STRATEGIC MEASURES AND BUSINESS PERFORMANCE: PIMS

PIMS stands for *Profit Impact of Market Strategy* and refers to an objective approach to analysing corporate performance using a unique database. Some 3,000 strategic business units (SBUs) have contributed over 20,000 years' experience to this database.

PIMS research on what drives business profits has become more widely known over the last 25 years as more evidence has become available. We know that there is, in general, a range of factors which we can quantify and relate to margins or to return on capital employed (ROCE). But does the evidence explain the spread between businesses in the same sector which dwarfs differences between industries?

PIMS results from examining real profits of real businesses suggest that the determinants of business performance can be grouped into four categories:

☐ market attractiveness;
☐ competitive strength;
☐ value-added structure;
☐ people and organization.

These are illustrated in Figure 7.6.

The first category contains factors relative to market attractiveness that affect an enterprises performance. Customer bargaining power, market complexity, market growth and innovation are obvious examples.

The second group describes how a business differs from its competitors in its market. Share position, customer preferences relative to competitors' offerings, market coverage and product range all have an effect.

The third category quantifies the way a business converts inputs into outputs; it includes investment intensity, fixed/working capital split, employee productivity, capacity use and vertical integration.

People and organization, an area in which PIMS has only recently built up comparable data, includes managers' attitudes, skill and training mix, personnel policies and incentives.

Figure 7.7 shows the impact of these factors on business profits tracked across PIMS's 3,000 businesses. Some factors are more important than others, but each has an influence that is both measurable and explainable. The positioning of a business on the chart can be described as its 'profile'.

To test whether the profile of a business can explain its profits, irrespective of the industry in which it operates, PIMS looked at the performance of businesses with 'weak' and 'strong' profiles in each of five sectors. Weak and strong profiles were picked in terms of position on each of the fifteen variables in Figure 7.8. Factors related to people and organization were omitted from the exercise

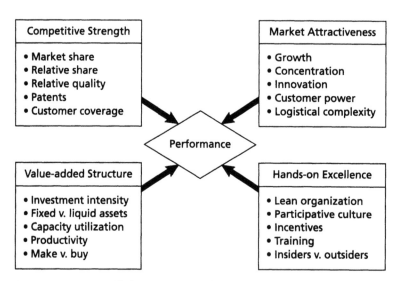

Figure 7.6 PIMS can quantify how strategic factors drive performance

Factor	−	Effect on ROCE	+
Market attractiveness			
Market growth	Low		High
Innovation	Zero, very high		Moderate
R&D spend	Zero, very high		Moderate
Marketing spend	High		Low
Contract size	Large		Small
Customer complexity	Complex		Simple
Competitive strength			
Relative share	Low		High
Relative quality	Worse		Better
Differentiation	Commodity		Differentiated
Customer spread	Narrow		Broader
Product range	Narrow		Broader
Value-added structure			
Investment/sales	High		Low
Capacity use	Low		High
Vertical integration	Low		High
Employee productivity	Low		High
People and organization			
Attitudes	Restrictive		Open
Training	Little		Substantial
Incentives	Weak		Strong

Figure 7.7 Impact of strategic factors on performance
(Source: PIMS database)

because the available sample at the time was not large enough to examine them by sector.

The results were startling! In every industry sector where there were enough observations to test, a business with a weak profit makes a 6 per cent return on sales (ROS) or 10 per cent ROCE over a four-year period. In contrast, a strong-profile business makes 11 per cent ROS or 30 per cent ROCE. The gap in profit performance between strong and weak businesses in each sector is bigger than the standard deviation in each group. So the profile does a better job of explaining differences in performance than the industry in which the business operates. The profile represents the strategic logic that shapes the real competitive choices facing managers in each business (see Figure 7.9).

These results are critically important. Earlier studies have shown how margins are related to business characteristics, but this is the first time that businesses in different industries with similar profiles have been shown to have more in common when it comes to performance than businesses in the same industry with different profiles.

PIMS also tested the relationships between margins and profile variables in various sub-sectors in the chemical industry, which is particularly well represented in the

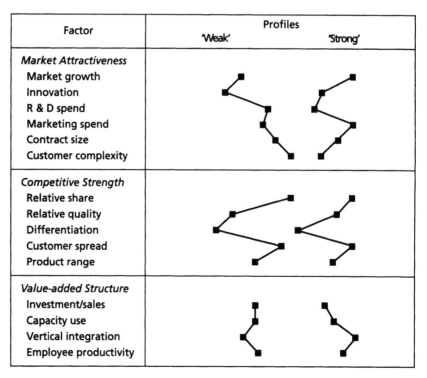

Figure 7.8 PIMS profiles – 1

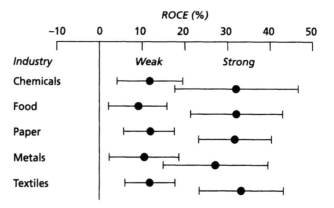

Figure 7.9 PIMS profiles – 2
(Source: PIMS database)

PIMS database. In each case the determinants included in the profile have a powerful, and consistent, influence on profits. The effect of each determinant is similar irrespective of the product category. This is true even for what is probably the most subjective of the variables which PIMS measures: relative quality.

7.4 SUMMARY

This chapter has focused on patterns of resource utilization and productivity by relating inputs to outputs via ratio analysis. From approaches such as this it is possible to diagnose the causes of variances between desired performance (as shown by target ratios) and actual performance (i.e. the values of ratios achieved). In this way managers can learn from the past to help them in moving towards a better future.

A ratio pyramid can be constructed which is specific to marketing activities – whether order-getting or order-filling.

A significant development that goes well beyond the traditional approach to ratio analysis is the PIMS approach. This comprises a high database which can be interrogated to identify determinants of superior corporate performance.

8 Variance analysis

LEARNING OBJECTIVES

After reading this chapter you should be able to:
- ☐ appreciate the role of variance analysis in securing control over marketing activities;
- ☐ recognize the importance of looking outwards to the marketplace in calculating variances;
- ☐ understand the need to distinguish between planning variances and performance variances.

8.1 INTRODUCTION

At their simplest, variances represent differences between an actual and a desired result, and they can relate to inputs or outputs. The role of variance analysis is to investigate the causes of variances that are deemed significant in order that any remedial actions that seem to be necessary can be prescribed. In identifying causes we are able to generate insights that enhance our understanding of organizational and market processes – in other words, we can learn.

It would be misguided to suppose that we only learn from things that go wrong since we can also learn from things that have gone better than anticipated. On these grounds we should not assume that favourable variances do not need to be investigated: if we are achieving more than we thought possible it is desirable to ascertain why this is so – and perhaps to do more of the same. On the other hand, if we are performing below par, it is also desirable to find out why – but to do even less.

8.2 SALES VARIANCES

When actual selling prices differ from standard selling prices a *sales price variance* can be computed. Standard selling prices will be used in compiling budgets, but it may be necessary to adapt to changing market conditions by raising or lowering prices, so it becomes desirable to segregate variances due to price changes from variances due to changes in quantity and product mix.

Quantity and mix are the two components of *sales volume variances*, and variations in profit can be explained to some extent by analysing sales quantity and sales mix. (Some writers – such as Malcom (1978), Bastable and Bao (1988) and Gibson (1990) – have argued that sales mix variances are potentially misleading, other than in specific situations.)

The formulae for computing sales variances are:

Sales price variance
  = Actual units sold × (Actual price − Standard price)

Sales volume variance
  = Sales quantity variance + Sales mix variance

Sales quantity variance
  = Budgeted profit on budgeted sales − Expected profit on actual sales

Sales mix variance
  = Expected profit on actual sales − Standard profit on actual sales.

'Expected profit on actual sales' is calculated as though profit increases or decreases proportionately with changes in the level of sales. 'Standard profit on actual sales' is the sum of the standard profit per unit for all units sold. (For a single-product enterprise, or in one where the profit per unit of sales is constant over the product range, the standard profit on actual sales is equal to the expected profit on actual sales, and the sales mix variance will necessarily be nil.)

Let us clarify the method with an example. Assume that the budgeted sales of a company's two products for a forthcoming period were as follows:

Product A 500 units at £2.00 per unit
Product B 700 units at £1.50 per unit

and their costs were:

Product A £1.75 per unit
Product B £1.30 per unit

Actual sales for the period were:

Product A 560 units at £1.95 per unit
Product B 710 units at £1.40 per unit

Budgeted sales revenue
  = £[(500 × 2.00) + (700 × 1.50)]   = £2,050
Actual sales revenue
  = £[(560 × 1.95) + (710 × 1.40)]   = £2,086

Budgeted profit
  = £[(500 × 0.25) + (700 × 0.20)] =   £265
Actual profit
  = £[(560 × 0.20) + (710 × 0.10)] =   £183
  Total sales variance   −£82
Sales price variance:
  = £[560 × (1.95 − 2.00)] + [710 × (1.40 − 1.50)] =   −£99

Sales volume variance:
　Quantity variance
　　= £265 − [2086/2050 × 265] =　　　　　　　　　+£4
　Mix variance
　　= £269 − [(560 × 0.25) + (710 × 0.20)] =　　　+£13
　Sales volume variance　　　　　　　　　　　　　　—　+£17

Total sales variance　　　　　　　　　　　　　　　　　−£82

8.3 MARKETING VARIANCES

It is clearly more difficult to establish precise standards for most marketing activities than is the case in the manufacturing or distribution functions. Physical and mechanical factors are less influential; psychological factors are more prominent; objective measurement is more limited; personal judgement is more conspicuous; tolerance limits must be broader; and the range of segments for which marketing standards can be developed is much greater. But the discipline of seeking to establish standards can generate insights into relationships between effort and results that are likely to outweigh any lack of precision.

It is possible for an organization to develop marketing standards by participation in an inter-firm comparison scheme (such as the one run by the Centre for Inter-firm Comparison). As Westwick (1987) has shown, integrated sets of ratios and standards can be devised to allow for detailed monitoring of marketing performance.

When budget levels and standards are being developed it is vitally important to note the assumptions on which they have been based since it is inevitable that circumstances will change and a variety of unanticipated events will occur once the budget is being implemented. Bearing this in mind, let us work through an example. Figure 8.1 illustrates an extract from a marketing plan for product X (column 2), with

Column 1 Item	Column 2 Plan	Column 3 Actual	Column 4 Variance
Revenues:			
Sales (units)	10,000,000	11,000,000	1,000,000
Price per unit (£)	1.00	0.95	0.05
Total revenue (£)	10,000,000	10,450,000	450,000
Market:			
Total market size (units)	25,000,000	30,000,000	5,000,000
Share of market (%)	40.0	36.7	(3.3)
Costs:			
Variable cost per unit (£)	0.60	0.60	—
Contribution:			
Per unit (£)	0.40	0.35	0.05
Total contribution	4,000,000	3,850,000	(150,000)

Figure 8.1 Operating results for product X
(Source: adapted from Hulbert and Toy 1977: 13)

actual results (column 3) and variances (column 4) being shown for a particular operating period.

The unfavourable contribution variance of £150,000 shown at the foot of column 4 is due to two principal causes:

1. a variance relating to sales volume; and
2. a variance relating to contribution per unit.

In turn, a variance relating to sales volume can be attributed to differences between:

3. actual and anticipated total market size; and
4. actual and anticipated market share.

Therefore a variation between planned and actual contribution may be due to variations in price per unit, variable cost per unit, total market size and market penetration.
    In the case of product X we have:

1. Profit variance
   $$(C_a - C_p) \times Q_a = £(0.35 - 0.40) \times 11,000,000$$
   $$= (£550,000)$$

2. Volume variance
   $$(Q_a - Q_p) \times C_p = (11,000,000 - 10,000,000) \times £0.40$$
   $$= £400,000$$

3. Net variance
Profit variance	£(550,000)
Volume variance	£400,000
	£(150,000)

where:

C_a = Actual contribution per unit
C_p = Planned contribution per unit
Q_a = Actual quantity sold in units
Q_p = Planned quantity of sales in units.

Figure 8.2 illustrates the relations.

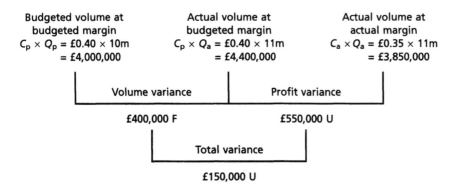

Figure 8.2 Marketing variances (1)

However, the volume variance (2 above) can be analysed further to take into account the impact of market size and penetration variations.

4. Market size variance
$(M_a - M_p) \times S_p \times C_p$
$= (30{,}000{,}000 - 25{,}000{,}000) \times 0.4 \times 0.4$
$= £800{,}000$
5. Market share variance
$(S_a - S_p) \times M_a \times C_p$
$= (0.367 - 0.40) \times 30{,}000{,}000 \times 0.4$
$= £(400{,}000)$
6. Volume variance

Market size variance	£800,000
Market share variance	£(400,000)
	£400,000

where:

M_a = Actual total market in units
M_p = Planned total market in units
S_a = Actual market share
S_p = Planned market share

See Figure 8.3, which illustrates these relationships.

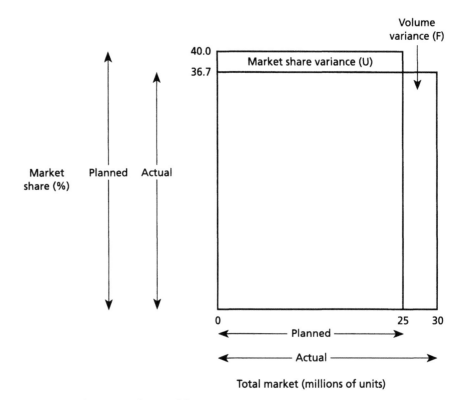

Figure 8.3 Marketing variances (2)

In summary, the position now appears thus:

Planned profit contribution		£4,000,000
Volume variance:		
Market size variance	£800,000	
Market share variance	£(400,000)	
		400,000
Profit variance		(550,000)
Actual profit contribution		£3,850,000

But this is not the end of the analysis! Variances arise because of unsatisfactory performance and unsatisfactory plans. It is desirable, therefore, to distinguish variances due to the poor execution of plans from those due to the poor establishing of plans. In the latter category are likely to be found forecasting errors reflecting faulty assumptions, and the estimates of total market size may constitute poor benchmarks for gauging subsequent managerial performance.

It is difficult to determine categorically whether market share variances are primarily the responsibility of forecasters or those who execute the plans based on forecasts. On the face of it the primary responsibility is likely to be attached to the latter group.

In interpreting the variances for product X it can be seen that the favourable volume variance of £400,000 resulted from two variances relating to market size and market share. Both of these are undesirable since they led to a lower contribution than intended. Had the forecasting group correctly anticipated the larger total market it should have been possible to devise a better plan to achieve the desired share and profit contribution. The actual outcome suggests that competitive position has been lost due to a loss of market share in a rapidly growing market. This is a serious pointer.

Lower prices resulted in a lower level of contribution per unit, and hence a lower overall profit contribution. The reasons for this need to be established and future plans modified as necessary.

As an approach to improved learning about the links between effort and results – especially in the face of active competitive behaviour – it is helpful to take the above analysis further and to evaluate performance by considering what should have happened in the circumstances (which is akin to flexible budgeting in a manufacturing setting).

At the end of the operating period to which Figure 8.1 refers it may become known that a large company with substantial resources made an aggressive entry into the marketplace using lots of promotions and low prices. Furthermore, an unforeseen export demand for product X may have arisen due to a prolonged strike in the USA's main manufacturer. On the basis of these details it becomes possible to carry out an *ex post* performance analysis in which the original plans are revised to take account of what has since become known. (See the discussion on p. 31 where this approach was first introduced.)

A clearer distinction can be made via *ex post* performance analysis along these lines since a distinction can be made between:

1. planning variances due to environmental events that were
   (a) foreseeable;
   (b) unforeseeable;
2. performance variances that are due to problems in executing the plans.

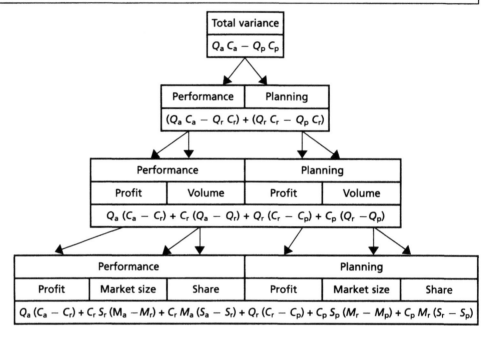

Legend

Subscripts	Variables
a = actual	Q = quantity
p = planned	C = contribution margins
r = revised	S = share
	M = market

Figure 8.4 *Ex post* performance analysis

The situation is summarized in Figure 8.4.

This example has focused on a single product line (product X), but multi-product companies will typically have product lines with differing cost structures and prices and hence profit characteristics. It will be apparent, therefore, that the *mix* of products sold will have an impact on the overall profit outcome. For example, an enterprise may offer three product lines with budgeted characteristics relating to the next operating period, as given in Figure 8.5.

	Product A	Product B	Product C	Total
Budget sales (units)	100,000	200,000	50,000	
Budgeted unit selling price	£12.00	£10.00	£20.00	
Budgeted unit variable cost	£6.00	£4.50	£8.00	
Budgeted unit contribution	£6.00	£5.50	£12.00	
Budgeted unit contribution	50%	55%	60%	
Budgeted contribution	£600,000	£1,100,000	£600,000	£2,300,000

Figure 8.5 Budgeted operating results by product line

	Product A	Product B	Product C	Total
Actual sales (units)	90,000	220,000	45,000	
Actual unit selling price	£12.00	£9.00	£20.00	
Actual unit variable cost	£6.00	£4.50	£9.00	
Actual unit contribution	£6.00	£4.50	£11.00	
Actual contribution	50%	50%	55%	
Actual contribution	£540,000	£990,000	£495,000	£2,025,000

Figure 8.6 Actual operating results by product line

Each product line has a different contribution per unit, so the total contribution from all lines is dependent upon the particular mix of sales across all product lines. If the actual outcomes for the period in question were as shown in Figure 8.6 we can explain the total variance of £275,000 U (i.e. actual profit contribution £2,025,000 minus budgeted profit contribution £2,300,000) as in Figure 8.7.

In summary we have:

	£
Volume variance	32,863 F
Mix variance	42,863 U
Profit variance	265,000 U
Total variance	£275,000 U

In other words, the total variance was partly due to overall volume being higher than budgeted (355,000 units rather than 350,000 as budgeted), which gives a favourable variance of £32,863 made up of favourable volume variances for each individual product line; the actual mix of sales differed from budget in a way that produced an unfavourable variance of £42,863 made up of unfavourable variances for products A and C which were partly offset by a favourable variance for product line B; and the actual margins were less than budgeted for product lines B and C, giving an unfavourable profit variance of £265,000.

The volume variance can be analysed further along the lines suggested in the previous example, but the main point to note from this example is the impact that variations in the mix of products sold can have on the profit outcome. If all product lines had the same percentage margin there would be no mix variance, but this situation is not normal, so we need to be aware of the impact of mix changes.

Let us now consider the frequency of reporting of variances (or other performance data). As a general proposition there are distinct benefits to be derived from minimizing the time lag between the occurrence of an event and the reporting of the outcome of that event. The validity of this assertion is derived from psychological learning theory from which it is evident that prompt feedback (or *knowledge of results*) serves to reinforce correct behaviour and to facilitate learning when outcomes are other than correct. Our everyday experience provides evidence of both of these aspects: when we do something right – and are informed that we have done it right – it boosts our confidence and demonstrates that we are capable of behaving in the desired manner. Conversely, when we have failed to produce the right outcome we

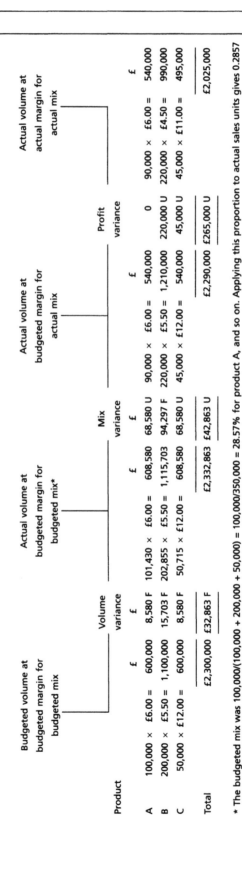

Product	Budgeted volume at budgeted margin for budgeted mix		Volume variance	Actual volume at budgeted margin for budgeted mix*		Mix variance	Actual volume at budgeted margin for actual mix		Profit variance	Actual volume at actual margin for actual mix	
		£	£		£	£		£	£		£
A	100,000 × £6.00 =	600,000	8,580 F	101,430 × £6.00 =	608,580	68,580 U	90,000 × £6.00 =	540,000	0	90,000 × £6.00 =	540,000
B	200,000 × £5.50 =	1,100,000	15,703 F	202,855 × £5.50 =	1,115,703	94,297 F	220,000 × £5.50 =	1,210,000	220,000 U	220,000 × £4.50 =	990,000
C	50,000 × £12.00 =	600,000	8,580 F	50,715 × £12.00 =	608,580	68,580 U	45,000 × £12.00 =	540,000	45,000 U	45,000 × £11.00 =	495,000
Total		£2,300,000	£32,863 F		£2,332,863	£42,863 U		£2,290,000	£265,000 U		£2,025,000

* The budgeted mix was 100,000/(100,000 + 200,000 + 50,000) = 100,000/350,000 = 28.57% for product A, and so on. Applying this proportion to actual sales units gives 0.2857 (90,000 + 220,000 + 45,000) = 101,430 for product A, and so on for B and C.

Note: F = favourable, U = unfavourable

Figure 8.7 Marketing variances (3)

need to be advised of this quickly in order that we might seek the correct answer and thereby learn to associate causes with effects (or actions with outcomes) more effectively in the future.

8.4 SUMMARY

The focus of this chapter has been on the analysis of variances as an approach that helps in feedback control.

Variances can be calculated wherever there is a difference between actual inputs or outputs and desired inputs or outputs. A common starting point is to identify an overall profit variance and then to seek to explain this (i.e. to identify the causal factors) by means of variance analysis. An array of sales and marketing variances can be generated to help in gaining insights as a basis for action.

There is a continuing debate within the literature over the most appropriate approach to variance analysis in a marketing context (see, for example, Shank and Churchill 1977; Hirsch 1988; Kauffman and Sopariwala 1995).

9 Marketing and distribution audits

LEARNING OBJECTIVES

After reading this chapter you should be able to:
- recognize the role of audits in securing control over marketing activities;
- understand how to set about an audit of marketing, distribution and retailing activities;
- appreciate the characteristics of an effective audit.

9.1 INTRODUCTION

Management auditing exists to appraise and review critically the firm's management process, covering the extent and effectiveness of the system of delegation, channels of communication, harmony of coordination, the adequacy of the methods of planning and control, the skill in supplying management information as a guide to action and, in general, the competence of supervisory and specialist teams.

This is a wide range of matters to review and appraise, but at all times the management auditor must bear in mind that he or she is not the manager: his or her function is to supply a service to management, and the auditor can only adequately discharge this service by remaining independent and free of executive responsibility. Nevertheless, it is vital that management auditors adopt a management perspective, lest they become obsessed with the accuracy of figures rather than with the managerial implications of inefficient practices.

A particularly significant development within the field of management auditing is the operational audit. This is totally removed from any financial audit concept, since the procedure is to select an activity for study, review and appraisal. The following are three examples: the marketing audit, the distribution audit and the retail audit.

9.2 AUDITS

The marketing audit

The marketing audit exists to help correct difficulties and to improve conditions that may already be good. While these aims may be achieved by a piece-meal examination of individual activities, they are better achieved by a total programme of evaluation studies. The former approach is termed a 'vertical audit' as it is only concerned with one element of the marketing mix at any one time. In contrast, the second approach, the 'horizontal audit', is concerned with optimizing the use of resources, thereby maximizing the total effectiveness of marketing efforts and outlays. As such, it is by far the more difficult of the two, and hence rarely attempted.

No matter which form of marketing audit is selected, top management (via its audit staff) should ensure that no area of marketing activity goes unevaluated, and that every aspect is evaluated in accordance with standards that are compatible with the overall success of the marketing organization and of the firm as a whole. This, of course, requires that all activities be related to the established hierarchy of objectives.

The auditing process should begin with agreement being reached between the organization's marketing director and the marketing auditor – someone from inside or outside the organization – regarding the specific objectives, the breadth and depth of coverage, the sources of data, the report format and the time period for the audit. Included within this should be a plan of who is to be interviewed and the questions that are to be asked.

With regard to the question of *who* is to be questioned, it needs to be emphasized that the audit should never be restricted to the company's executives; it should also include customers, the dealer network, relevant employees and other outside groups. In this way, a better and more complete picture of the company's position and its effectiveness can be developed. In the case of customers and dealers, for example, the auditor should aim to develop satisfaction ratings that are capable of highlighting areas in need of attention.

Once the information has been collected, the findings and recommendations need to be presented with emphasis being given to the type of action needed to overcome any problems, the time scale over which remedial action is to be taken, and the names of those who are to be responsible for this.

Within the general framework of the external and internal audits, Kotler *et al.* (1989) suggest there are six specific dimensions that are of direct interest to the auditor. These are:

1. The *marketing environment audit*, which involves an analysis of the major macroeconomic forces and trends within the organization's task environment. This includes markets, customers, competitors, distributors, dealers and suppliers.
2. The *marketing strategy audit*, which focuses upon a review of the organization's marketing objectives and strategy, with a view to determining how well suited they are to the current and forecasted market environment.
3. The *marketing organization audit*, which follows on from the previous aspect and is concerned specifically with an evaluation of the structural capability of the organization and its suitability for implementing the strategy needed for the developing environment.

4. The *marketing systems audit*, which covers the quality of the organization's systems for analysis, planning and control.
5. The *marketing productivity audit*, which examines the profitability of different aspects of the marketing programme and the cost effectiveness of various levels of marketing expenditure.
6. The *marketing functions audit* involving a detailed evaluation of each of the elements of the marketing mix.

The distribution audit

In the planning and control of costs and effectiveness in distribution activities the management audit can be of considerable value. Not surprisingly, however, it entails a complex set of procedures right across the function if it is to be carried out thoroughly. The major components are the channel audit, the physical distribution management (PDM) audit, the competitive audit and the customer service audit. Each of these will be considered briefly in turn.

(a) The channel audit

Channels are made up of the intermediaries (such as wholesalers, factors, retailers) through which goods pass on their route from manufacture to consumption. The key channel decisions include:

- choosing intermediaries;
- determining the implications (from a physical distribution point of view) of alternative channel structures; and
- assessing the available margins.

It follows from the nature of these decisions that the main focus of a channel audit will be on structural factors on the one hand and on cost/margin factors on the other.

(b) The PDM audit

There are three primary elements within this audit: that of company profile (which includes the handling cost characteristics of the product range and the service level that is needed in the light of market conditions); PDM developments (both of a technological and of a contextual nature); and that of the current system's capability.

Cost aspects exist in each of these elements, but operating costs loom largest in the last since it is predominantly concerned with costs and capacity. For example, some of the items that will be subjected to audit will include those shown in Figure 9.1.

(c) The competitive audit

Through this phase it should be possible to ascertain the quality of competitors' distribution policies, practices and facilities, and especially the level of service that competitors are able to offer (and maintain). Within the competitive audit regard should also be paid to channel structures, pricing and discount policies and market shares.

Capacity utilization	— Warehouse
	— Transportation
	— Flexibility and expansion scope
Warehouse facilities	— Total costs
	— Age and maintenance costs
	— Flexibility throughout/period
	— Total throughout/period
	— Returns handled — number
	— recovery time
	— Picking accuracy
	— Service levels/back orders
	— Cube utilization
	— Cost of cube bought out
Inventory	— Total inventory holding costs
	— Product group costs
	— Service levels — total
	— plant
	— field
	— Field inventory holding costs
	— Transfers — number
	— volume
	— Stockout effects — loss of business
	— rectification costs
Transportation	— Total costs
	— Production to field units
	— Field units to customers
	— Vehicle utilization
	— Vehicle cube utilization
	— Total volumes shipped
	— Cost per mile — volumes shipped
	— cases/pallets shipped
	— Costs of service bought out
	— Costs by mode/comparisons
Communications	— Total costs
	— Order communication times — method
	— cost
	— Time and costs per line item per order method for:
	— order processing and registration
	— credit investigation
	— invoice and delivery note preparation
	— statement preparation

Figure 9.1 System capability factors

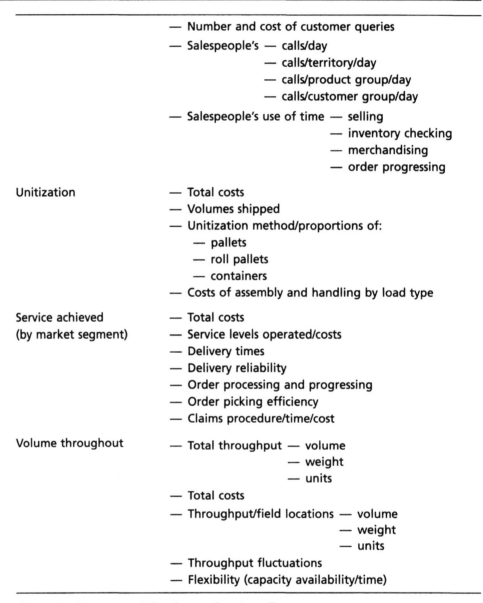

	— Number and cost of customer queries
	— Salespeople's — calls/day
	— calls/territory/day
	— calls/product group/day
	— calls/customer group/day
	— Salespeople's use of time — selling
	— inventory checking
	— merchandising
	— order progressing
Unitization	— Total costs
	— Volumes shipped
	— Unitization method/proportions of:
	— pallets
	— roll pallets
	— containers
	— Costs of assembly and handling by load type
Service achieved (by market segment)	— Total costs
	— Service levels operated/costs
	— Delivery times
	— Delivery reliability
	— Order processing and progressing
	— Order picking efficiency
	— Claims procedure/time/cost
Volume throughout	— Total throughput — volume
	— weight
	— units
	— Total costs
	— Throughput/field locations — volume
	— weight
	— units
	— Throughput fluctuations
	— Flexibility (capacity availability/time)

Figure 9.1 System capability factors (continued)

(d) The customer service audit

Given that the level of service is at the centre of physical distribution management it is essential to monitor regularly its cost and quality characteristics.

A very thorough approach to the distribution audit is that developed at the Cranfield School of Management by Martin Christopher and his colleagues.

The retail audit

As in marketing and distribution, the management audit can be developed to evaluate retail activities. The main steps of a retail audit are shown in Figure 9.2. These consist of the following:

1. *Determining who is to do the audit.* There are basically three possibilities:
   (a) company specialists (i.e. internal auditors with particular expertise in retail and in the organization in question;
   (b) departmental managers on a do-it-yourself basis; and
   (c) outside specialists on a consulting basis.
   The relative costs, degree of objectivity and expertise, plus the scope for combining 'vertical' audits into a 'horizontal' one will influence the choice.
2. *Determining when and how often the audit is to be conducted.* Various 'obvious' times suggest themselves (see Figure 9.2). Annual audits are, however, rather too infrequent to be of significant operational benefit.
3. *Determining which areas are to be audited.* In other words, should the audit be specific to one factor ('vertical') or an across-the-board assessment ('horizontal')?
4. *Developing the audit forms.* These detailed questionnaires should cover all the aspects worthy of investigation (given the aims of the audit). Examples will be given later in this section – see Figures 9.3–5.
5. *Carrying out the audit.* A number of important questions arise in this phase of the audit (as shown in Figure 9.2).
6. *Reporting to management.* Once the audit has been completed it is essential to present the findings (with appropriate recommendations) to management. It is only as a result of managerial decisions based on a carefully prepared report that action leading to improvements in cost control procedures is likely.

In proceeding through these stages it is inevitable that a number of problems will be met. Not least of all the audit will be expensive, in terms both of money and time, but there are human problems (such as individuals' feeling threatened by investigations) and problems of data availability and accuracy to contend with.

To give a clearer indication of how one might develop a retail audit the questionnaires shown in Figures 9.3-5 offer suggestions relating to small retailers' activities. Figure 9.3 focuses on budgetary and productivity issues, Figure 9.4 on cash and finance, and Figure 9.5 on credit policies. Similar questionnaires can be developed for customer relations, personnel management, stock control, purchasing, pricing, advertising and promotion, display equipment and layout, and many other aspects of a small retailer's activities. Collectively, a set of questionnaires developed along these lines will facilitate a systematic, horizontal audit.

The specific needs of large retailers will need to be met by questionnaires designed especially to suit their organizational and operational characteristics.

Other examples of operational audits would include the purchasing function, covering the full spectrum of activities and procedures from the time an item is required and ordered until it is finally received, paid for, and charged to expense in the accounts.

The integral aspects of the study would include:

☐ the factors required for effective purchasing
☐ cooperation and coordination with other departments

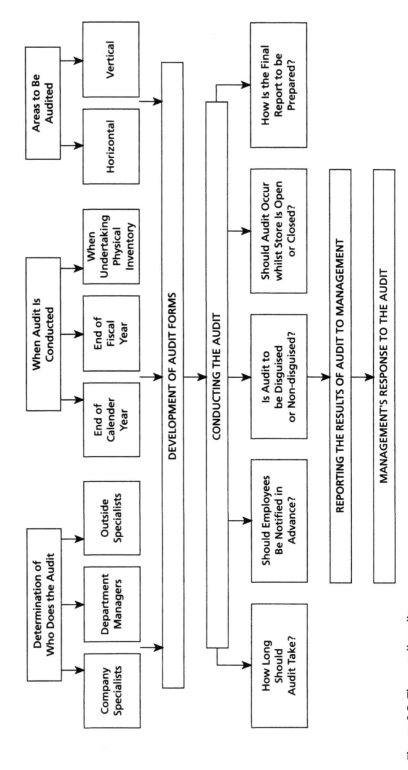

Figure 9.2 The retail audit process

> 1 Do you express your plans in terms of a budget, covering sales, stocks, mark-ups and expenses?
> 2 Do you set up your budget for relatively short periods?
> 3 Do you make an organized effort to determine the potential sales of your merchandise lines in your community and to calculate your market share?
> 4 In controlling your operations, do you frequently compare actual results with the budget projections you have made; and do you then adjust your merchandising, promotion and expense plans as indicated by deviations from these projections?
> 5 Do your key employees have a voice in formulating budget plans concerning them?
> 6 Do you study industry data and compare the results of your operation with them?
> 7 Do you think in terms of ratios and percentages, rather than exclusively in pounds and pence?
> 8 Do you use a variety of measures of productivity, such as:
>   (a) net profit as percentage of your net worth;
>   (b) stockturn (ratio of cost of your sales to the value of your average inventory);
>   (c) gross profit margin per pound of cost investment in merchandise (pounds of gross margin divided by your average inventory at cost);
>   (d) sales per square metre of space (net sales divided by total number of square metres of space); and
>   (e) selling cost per cent for each salesperson (remunerations of the salesperson divided by that person's sales)?

Figure 9.3 Management for small retailers: budgetary control and productivity

- controls
- purchase authorization
- selection of suppliers
- negotiation of terms
- issue of official purchase orders
- follow-up of order
- receipt and inspection of delivered goods
- stores procedures.

Similarly, studies can be done on the efficiency and weaknesses of every function in the company, and should lead to cost savings and profit improvement in all cases.

Although similar to O & M studies in some respects, operational audits are concerned with improvements in managerial processes rather than purely paper flows. They are more comprehensive than other forms of control, but nevertheless are best used as supplementary control devices, and not as primary ones.

As with marketing research and operations research studies, the initial outcome of the management audit is a report. If this is poorly written, or fails to include all pertinent details, it may cause damaging decisions to be made. The need for skill and patience in drawing up reports can hardly be exaggerated, as the overall effectiveness of any study depends mainly upon the report, the distribution it receives, and the effectiveness of the follow-up action.

1 Does someone other than the cashier or book-keeper open all mail and prepare a record of receipts that will be checked against deposits?

2 Do you deposit all of each day's cash receipts in the bank without delay?

3 Do you restrict the use of your petty cash funds to payment of small expenditures (not exceeding a stated amount) and limit them to the amount needed for a short period of time – a week or two?

4 Do you require adequate identification of 'cash-take' customers who want to pay by cheque and those who ask you to cash cheques?

5 Have you taken adequate steps to protect your cash from robbery?

6 Is your postage metered?

7 Are your cheques prenumbered?

8 Are you careful to lay aside cash for all amounts withheld from employees' wages for taxes, national insurance, etc., and for all VAT collected and to remit these sums as required to the appropriate authorities?

9 Do you calculate your cash flow regularly (monthly, for example) and take steps to provide enough cash for each period's needs?

10 Have you established, in advance, a line of credit at your bank, not only to meet seasonal requirements but also to permit borrowing at any time for emergency needs?

11 Do you consistently avoid drawing cheques to 'cash' and signing blank cheques?

12 Have you taken out indemnity insurance on your cashier and other employees who handle cash and securities?

13 Do you keep company securities under lock and key, preferably in a safe deposit vault?

14 Do you control your liabilities with the same degree of care you devote to your assets?

15 To permit modernization and expansion of your premises (if you rent them), have you seriously considered your landlord as a source for the additional capital you will need?

16 Do you maintain a close personal relationship with your local bank?

Figure 9.4 Management for small retailers: cash and finance

1 Do you have a credit policy?

2 Do you set definite credit limits and explain your rules carefully to all credit applicants?

3 When customers do not make payments as agreed, do you follow up promptly?

4 If you have your own credit plan, do you have a simple method of identifying credit customers and authorizing their purchases?

5 Have you introduced a revolving credit plan whereby customers can complete payment for merchandise by means of a number of monthly, or weekly, payments and are privileged to buy more at any time within a set limit?

6 Are your bad debt losses comparable with those of other similar stores?

7 Periodically, do you review your accounts to determine their status?

8 Are you a member of a retail credit bureau, and do you actively use the information it provides?

Figure 9.5 Management for small retailers: credit

9.3 THE CHARACTERISTICS OF EFFECTIVE AUDITS

Four dimensions can be highlighted in seeking to characterize an effective audit. These are that it should be comprehensive, systematic, independent and periodic. Let us consider each of these in a little more detail (after Kotler 1988).

(a) Comprehensive

For the auditing process to be worthwhile it is essential that it cover *all* of the major elements of the organization's marketing activities, including those that seemingly are doing well, rather than just a few apparent trouble spots. In this way a distinction can be drawn between the *marketing audit* and a *functional audit* which would focus far more specifically upon a particular element of marketing activity such as sales or pricing. As an example of this, a functional audit might well suggest that a high sales-force turnover and low morale is due to a combination of inadequate sales training and a poor compensation package. A more fundamental reason, however, might be that the company has a poor or inadequate product range and an inappropriate pricing and advertising strategy. It is the comprehensiveness of the marketing audit that is designed to reveal these sorts of factors and to highlight the *fundamental* causes of the organization's problems.

(b) Systematic

In carrying out the audit it is essential that a sequential diagnostic process be adopted covering the three areas to which reference was made earlier: the external environment, internal marketing systems and specific marketing activities. This process of diagnosis is then followed by the development *and implementation* of both short-term and long-term plans designed to correct the weaknesses identified and, in this way, improve upon levels of marketing effectiveness.

(c) Independent

As with a financial audit, there are several ways in which the marketing audit can be conducted. These include:

- a self-audit in which managers use a checklist to assess their own results and methods of operation;
- an audit by a manager of the same status but drawn from a different department or division within the organization;
- an audit by a more senior manager within the same department or division;
- the use of a company auditing office;
- a company task force audit group;
- an audit conducted by an outside specialist.

Of these it is generally recognized that an audit conducted by an outside specialist is likely to prove the most objective and to exhibit the independence that any internal process will almost inevitably lack. Adopting this approach should also ensure that the audit receives the undivided time and attention that is needed. In practice, however, many large companies make use of their own audit teams (something which 3M, for example, has pioneered).

This question of *who* should conduct the audit has been the subject of a considerable amount of research and discussion in recent years with, as indicated above, the argument revolving around the issue of objectivity (in other words, how objective can a line manager be in conducting an evaluation of activities for which he or she has direct responsibility?). It is largely because of this that it has been suggested that outside consultants should be used to ensure impartiality. This is likely to prove expensive if done annually, and the answer is increasingly being seen to lie in a compromise whereby an outside consultant is used every third or fourth year, with line managers from different departments or divisions being used in the intervening periods. Alternatively an organization might opt for what is in essence a composite approach, with an external auditor being used initially to validate line managers' self-audits, and subsequently to integrate them to produce an audit result for the marketing function as a whole.

To a large extent, however, it can be argued that the supposed difficulties of achieving impartiality are overstated since a sufficiently well-structured and institutionalized auditing process can overcome many of these difficulties. There is a need, therefore, for managers to be trained in how best to use auditing procedures and, very importantly, for the audit process to be endorsed by senior management: without top management commitment to the audit process and, in turn, to the need to act on the results that emerge, the entire exercise is likely to prove valueless.

(d) Periodic

If the company is to benefit fully from the auditing process it is essential that it be carried out on a regular basis. All too often in the past companies have been spurred into conducting an audit largely as the result of poor performance. Ironically, this poor performance can often be traced to a myopia on the part of management, stemming from a failure to review activities on a sufficiently regular basis, something that was pointed to by Shuchman (1950), who commented that 'No marketing operation is ever so good that it cannot be improved. Even the best *must* be better, for few if any marketing operations can remain successful over the years by maintaining the status quo.'

9.4 SUMMARY

Within this chapter the focus has been on marketing, distribution and retail audits as means to facilitate feedback control.

Management audits in general seek to give a basis for improving performance that may already be good, and can be undertaken in a horizontal (i.e. comprehensive) or vertical (i.e. partial) way. We considered the central features of audits dealing with marketing, distribution and retail activities.

The characteristics of effective audits were identified (i.e. they should be comprehensive, systematic, independent and periodic).

Part 4

Cases and Exercises

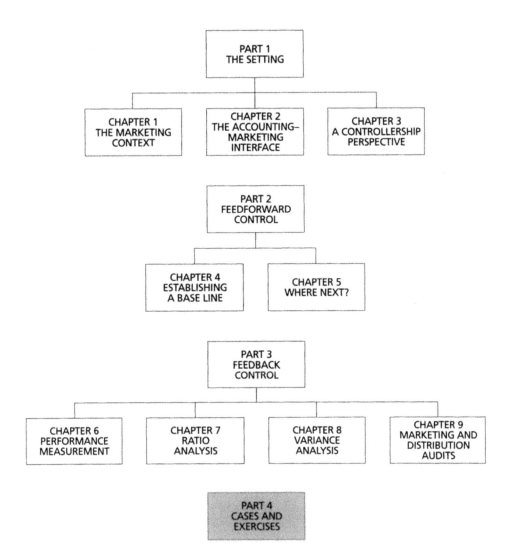

PART 1
THE SETTING

CHAPTER 1
THE MARKETING
CONTEXT

CHAPTER 2
THE ACCOUNTING–
MARKETING
INTERFACE

CHAPTER 3
A CONTROLLERSHIP
PERSPECTIVE

PART 2
FEEDFORWARD
CONTROL

CHAPTER 4
ESTABLISHING
A BASE LINE

CHAPTER 5
WHERE NEXT?

PART 3
FEEDBACK
CONTROL

CHAPTER 6
PERFORMANCE
MEASUREMENT

CHAPTER 7
RATIO
ANALYSIS

CHAPTER 8
VARIANCE
ANALYSIS

CHAPTER 9
MARKETING AND
DISTRIBUTION
AUDITS

PART 4
CASES AND
EXERCISES

INTRODUCTION

The material in Part 4 is intended to give readers an opportunity to reinforce and apply some of the ideas and approaches covered in Parts 1–3. There are three sections in this part of the book, dealing with discussion questions, exercises and case studies.

Discussion questions

QUESTION 1

(a) What do you understand by the notion of 'financial position'?
(b) In what ways is it relevant to marketing?

QUESTION 2

The profit and loss account has a particular attraction for most users of accounts in that it reports a 'bottom line' figure – the profit or loss for the financial year – which can be used as a shorthand performance measure.

Explain the limitations from the point of view of marketing management of conventional profit and loss accounts.

QUESTION 3

Why is the total cost concept helpful in managing physical distribution activities?

QUESTION 4

Which measures of profit are most useful to marketing managers? Justify your choice.

QUESTION 5

Explain how an enterprise's financial position might affect its marketing activities. Illustrate your answer with relevant examples.

QUESTION 6

Discuss the financial issues that arise in the process of developing and launching new products.

QUESTION 7

(a) Distinguish and define clearly the categories of costs that are appropriate for:
   (i) planning
   (ii) decision-making
   (iii) control.
(b) Give marketing examples applicable to each category.

QUESTION 8

What would you consider to be the best organizational arrangements within a company to ensure that the marketing function receives appropriate financial information and advice?

QUESTION 9

Explore the role of cost analysis in the pricing decision for:

(a) a fast-moving consumer product in a highly competitive market;
(b) a specialized industrial service.

QUESTION 10

(a) Distinguish between 'liquidity' and 'profitability'.
(b) Which is likely to be of greater significance to marketing decision-makers?

QUESTION 11

What patterns are to be found in the financial flows that are typically associated with the product life cycle?

QUESTION 12

Explain why the noun 'cost' can be misleading when used without a qualifying adjective.
   Give marketing examples to illustrate your answer.

QUESTION 13

(a) Explain the way in which cost centres, profit centres and investment centres might operate within a responsibility accounting system.

(b) Which type of responsibility centre (i.e. cost centre, profit centre or investment centre) would you recommend for each of the following:
   (i) marketing director
   (ii) distribution manager
   (iii) sales manager?

Justify your recommendations.

QUESTION 14

(a) To what extent do you think that financial ratios adequately function as measures of organizational performance?
(b) Suggest some ratios that you consider to be useful in evaluating marketing performance, and show how these ratios might be used.

QUESTION 15

Assume that you are the marketing director of a divisionalized company in the leisure industry. The divisions supply gardening equipment, seeds, garden furniture, etc., to a variety of distributive outlets.

(a) If your current concern is with divisional performance appraisal (primarily, but not exclusively, in financial terms), which performance measures might be of most interest to you?
(b) Assess the strengths and weaknesses of the measures you have discussed in (a) above.

QUESTION 16

(a) Identify the major categories of assets that are of interest to marketing managers.
(b) Why is it that published financial reports fail to include details of some assets that are of major interest to marketing managers?

QUESTION 17

A large company's advertising manager has requested board approval to increase this year's advertising budget by £50,000. The advertising manager believes that this extra outlay will increase sales during the year by £300,000. As marketing director, and a member of the board, what other information would you require in order to assess the request?

Exercises

EXERCISE 1

Pennine Ltd. manufactures soft drinks which are sold to retailers in cases of 12 bottles for £7.20, with Pennine's direct costs being £3.00 per case. The retailers' margin is 15p per bottle.

A special promotion is being considered by the marketing manager of Pennine. This is planned to last 4 months and involves a reduction in the retail price of 5p per bottle. The retailers will still receive their margin of 15p, and additional direct costs to Pennine of this promotion are estimated at 25p per case.

Forecast sales (in thousands of cases) are:

Month	1	2	3	4
With promotion	120	130	140	120
Without promotion	100	100	100	100

(a) Should the promotion go ahead?

(b) How would your recommendation in (a) change under either of the following independent circumstances?

    (i) Sales in month 3 are estimated at 130,000 cases if the promotion is undertaken.

    (ii) The additional direct costs of the promotion are expected to be 30p per case.

EXERCISE 2

The management of *Arnold & Co.* realizes that additional marketing/distribution cost studies are needed, but the company lacks the personnel and funds at present to establish accurate cost standards. They do, however, believe that they may be accepting too many small orders. As a result, they analyse the order sizes received last year and break their orders down by the simple categories of small (1–20 items), medium (21–100 items) and large (over 100 items). The actual marketing and distribution costs incurred last year and the bases for their apportionment are shown below:

Cost	Amount (£)	Basis for apportionment
Marketing personnel salaries	135,000	Number of personnel
Marketing manager's salary	30,000	Time spent
Salespersons' commissions	37,500	Value of sales
Advertising and direct selling	150,000	Value of sales
Packing and shipping	73,500	Weight shipped
Delivery	42,000	Weight shipped
Credit and collection	34,000	Number of orders

An analysis of their records produced the following statistics:

	Order size			
	Small	Medium	Large	Total
Number of personnel	5	3	1	9
Time spent by marketing manager	60%	10%	30%	100%
Value of sales (£)	250,000	300,000	200,000	750,000
Weight shipped	6,090	2,940	1,470	10,500
Number of orders	612	170	68	850

Required

(a) Prepare a detailed schedule showing the marketing cost per order size and marketing cost as a percentage of total sales for each order size.
(b) Interpret your answer to (a) with particular reference to the recommendations you would make to management regarding the size of order they should accept.

EXERCISE 3

The *Malone Company* manufactures and markets three products, A, B and C. Total sales revenue from all lines last year (to 30 April 1999) was £2,000,000. Product A is sold to a single customer under a long-term contract by which the customer purchases 5,000 units per month with an increase in unit price of 5 per cent per year.

The sales of products B and C are seasonal, as shown in the schedule (in units) for the year that has just ended.

During last year the unit selling price of product B was £2.00, whilst total sales of product C amounted to £1,200,000 at a constant unit price.

It is expected that:

☐ the seasonal pattern of last year will continue through next year;
☐ the selling price of product B will be increased by 10%, whilst the volume of sales of B is expected to fall by 10,000 units;
☐ the selling price of product C will be decreased by £1.00 per unit, with an increase in volume of 20%.

Month	Product B	Product C
May	1,000	3,000
June	2,000	6,000
July	3,000	6,000
August	5,000	6,000
September	8,000	3,000
October	12,000	3,000
November	24,000	3,000
December	18,000	3,000
January	9,000	15,000
February	7,000	30,000
March	6,000	45,000
April	5,000	27,000
	100,000	150,000

Required: Prepare a sales budget by product line and by month for the next quarter (i.e. May–July).

EXERCISE 4

Primrose Products is proposing to launch a new product to which the following data applies:

Estimated annual sales volume: 100,000 units @ £25.00
Estimated annual fixed costs:
    Marketing   £200,000
    Administration   £50,000
    Production   £350,000
Estimated variable costs:
    Selling, etc.   £2.00 per unit
    Manufacturing   £8.00 per unit
Estimated average investment in the product: £3,600,000
Target return: 25% ROI

Assume that the product has been launched and, eight months following the launch, it seems likely that annual sales will be 80,000 units for the next few years.

However, a major mail order firm has offered to buy 20,000 units per annum over the next 3 years at £15 per unit.

Required: As the sales manager of Primrose Products, would you accept this order? Justify your decision and make explicit the assumptions on which it is based.

EXERCISE 5

Acklam Ltd. sells its products in four territories for which the following budgets have been prepared to cover the final quarter of 1999:

	Territory			
	1	2	3	Total
Sales revenue	£400,000	£600,000	£200,000	£1,200,000
Salespersons' salaries	30,000	45,000	15,000	90,000
Travelling expenses	5,000	18,000	4,000	27,000
Warehousing expenses	3,000	6,000	2,000	11,000
Transportation expenses	4,000	15,000	2,000	21,000

It is estimated that the cost of sales will amount to 60% of sales value. Other expenses are estimated as follows:

Salespersons' commissions:	8% of sales value
Sales administration salaries:	£36,000
Sales office expenses:	£24,000
Credit and collection expenses:	1% of sales value
Advertising:	5% of sales value

Required:
(a) Using whatever assumptions you consider appropriate, and making your assumptions explicit, prepare a projected project statement for the quarter for each sales territory.
(b) Assess the usefulness of your answer to (a) from a managerial viewpoint.

EXERCISE 6

Deakin & Co. are engaged in marketing three products, A, B and C, in four sales regions. During January 2000, the sales volume, unit selling price and gross margin of each product were as follows:

	A	B	C
Sales (units)	12,000	18,000	30,000
Selling price (£)	60	25	15
Gross margin (%)	55	50	45
Kilos shipped	90,000	50,000	60,000

Order-getting and order-filling costs for the month were:

Personal selling	£260,000
Advertising	90,000
Transportation	120,000
Warehousing and handling	80,000
General	50,000

Certain additional information is available:

	Sales region			
	North	South	East	West
Shipments (units)				
Product A	2,000	2,500	3,000	4,500
Product B	6,000	2,000	6,000	4,000
Product C	9,000	6,000	7,000	8,000
Advertising effort	15%	25%	40%	20%
Sales calls	20%	15%	30%	35%

Required: Prepare a net profit statement showing the relative profit performance of each sales region for January 2000. Make whatever assumptions you feel to be necessary, but state (and justify) all the assumptions you have made.

EXERCISE 7

Strines & Co. is engaged in marketing three products, X, Y and Z. During November 1999, the sales volume, unit selling price and gross margin of each product were as follows:

	X	Y	Z
Sales (units)	10,000	15,000	25,000
Selling price (£)	50	20	10
Gross margin (%)	45	50	55

Order-getting and order-filling costs for the month were:

Personal selling	£180,000
Advertising	70,000
Transportation	90,000
Warehousing and handling	60,000
General	37,500

Certain additional information is available:

	X	Y	Z
Kilos shipped	90,000	50,000	60,000
Salespersons' time	20%	45%	35%
Advertising effort	40%	25%	35%

Required: Prepare a profit statement showing the relative profit performance of each product line for the month of November 1999.
Make whatever assumptions you feel to be necessary, but state (and justify) all the assumptions you have made.

EXERCISE 8

The *Merry Merchants Company* employs four salespersons, each covering a large territory. A basic salary of £800 per month is paid, plus a commission at the rate of 1% of sales revenue. All the salespersons have expense accounts to cover travelling and entertaining.

Additional data relating to December 1999 is given below:

	Salesperson			
	Graham	Alicia	Karen	Dick
Days on the road	22	22	22	22
Miles travelled	2,200	3,000	2,800	4,000
Calls made	88	110	66	72
Sales revenue	£200,000	£160,000	£180,000	£240,000
Travelling expenses	£330	£440	£390	£510
Entertaining expenses	£200	£300	£400	£600

Required: Assume the role of the company's sales manager. Write a report to the marketing director evaluating the performance of each salesperson for the month of December 1999.

EXERCISE 9

The following data relates to the most recent quarter's results for *Eaton Enterprises*:

	Actual	Budget
Sales (units)	180,000	200,000
Selling price per unit (£)	25	30
Sales revenue (£)	4,500,000	6,000,000

Required:
(a) Calculate
   (i) sales price variance;
   (ii) sales volume variance; and
   (iii) total sales variance for the period.
(b) Explain in broad terms how you would proceed to establish cost, revenue and profit standards relating to marketing activities.

EXERCISE 10

(a) The following data relate to Product X for last month:

	Budget	Actual	Variance
Sales	£990,000	£800,000	£190,000
Units sold	110,000	100,000	
Unit price	£9.00	£8.00	

Explain the variance of £190,000.

(b) How might a manager establish the significance of variances? Why is it important that this be done?

Case studies

CASE STUDY 1

The Peanut Seller

Joe, the restaurateur, adds a rack of peanuts to the counter, hoping to pick up a little extra profit in the usual course of business. He is interviewed by his accountant–efficiency expert.

Eff. Ex.: Joe, you said you put in these peanuts because some people ask for them, but do you realize what this rack of peanuts is costing you?

Joe: It ain't gonna cost, 'sgonna be a profit. Sure, I hadda pay $25 for a fancy rack to holda bags, but the peanuts cost 6c a bag and I sell 'em for 10c. Figger I sell 50 bags a week to start. It'll take 12½ weeks to cover the cost of the rack. After that I gotta clear profit of 4c a bag. The more I sell, the more I make.

Eff. Ex.: That is an antiquated and completely unrealistic approach, Joe. Fortunately, modern accounting procedures permit a more accurate picture which reveals the complexities involved.

Joe: Huh?

Eff. Ex.: To be precise, those peanuts must be integrated into your entire operation and be allocated their appropriate share of business overhead. They must share a proportionate part of your expenditures for rent, heat, light, equipment depreciation, decorating, salaries for your waitresses, cook –

Joe: The cook? What'sa he gotta do wit'a peanuts? He don't even know I got 'em!

Eff. Ex.: Look, Joe, the cook is in the kitchen, the kitchen prepares the food, the food is what brings people in here, and the people ask to buy peanuts. That's why you must charge a portion of the cook's wages, as well as part of your own salary to peanut sales. This sheet contains a carefully calculated costs analysis which indicates the peanut operation should pay exactly $1,278 per year toward these general overhead costs.

Joe: The peanuts? $1,278 a year for overhead? That's nuts!

Eff. Ex.: It's really a little more than that. You also spend money each week to have the windows washed, to have the place swept out in the mornings and to keep soap in the washroom. That raises the total to $1,313 per year.

Joe: (thoughtfully) But the peanut salesman said I'd make money – put 'em on the end of the counter, he said – and get 4c a bag profit.

Eff. Ex.: (with a sniff) He's not an accountant. Do you actually know what the portion of the counter occupied by the peanut rack is worth to you?

Joe: Ain't worth nothing – no stool there – just a dead spot at the end.

Eff. Ex.: The modern cost picture permits no dead spots. Your counter contains 60 square feet and your counter business grosses $15,000 a year. Consequently, the square foot of space occupied by the peanut rack is worth $250 per year. Since you have taken that area away from general counter use, you must charge the value of the space to the occupant.

Joe: You mean I gotta add $250 a year more to the peanuts?

Eff. Ex.: Right. That raises their share of the general operating costs to a grand total of $1,563 per year. Now then, if you sell 50 bags of peanuts per week, these allocated costs will amount to 60c per bag.

Joe: What?

Eff. Ex.: Obviously, to that must be added your purchase price of 6c per bag, which brings the total to 66c. So you see, by selling peanuts at 10c per bag you are losing 56c on every sale.

Joe: Somethin's crazy!

Eff. Ex.: Not at all! Here are the figures. They prove your peanut operation cannot stand on its own feet.

Joe: (brightening) Suppose I sell lotsa peanuts – thousand bags a week 'stead of fifty?

Eff. Ex.: (tolerantly) Joe, you don't understand the problem. If the volume of peanut sales increases, your operating costs will go up – you'll have to handle more bags, with more time, more depreciation, more everything. The basic principle of accounting is firm on that subject! 'The Bigger the Operation the More General Overhead Costs that Must be Allocated.' No, increasing the volume of sales won't help.

Joe: Okay. You so smart, you tell me what I gotta do.

Eff. Ex.: (condescendingly) Well – you could first reduce operating expenses.

Joe: How?

Eff. Ex.: Move to a building with cheaper rent. Cut salaries. Wash the windows bi-weekly. Have the floor swept only on Thursday. Remove the soap from the washrooms. Decrease the square foot value of your counter. For example, if you can cut your expenses 50 per cent, that will reduce the amount allocated to peanuts from $1,563 to $781.50 per year, reducing the cost to 36c per bag.

Joe: (slowly) That's better?

Eff. Ex.: Much, much better. However, even then you would lose 26c per bag, if you charge only 10c. Therefore, you must also raise your selling price. If you want a net profit of 4c per bag you would have to charge 40c.

Joe: (flabbergasted) You mean even after I cut operating costs 50 per cent, I still gotta charge 40c for a 10c bag of peanuts? Nobody's that nuts about nuts! Who'd buy em?

Eff. Ex.: That's a secondary consideration. The point is, at 40c you'd be selling at a price based upon a true and proper evaluation of your then reduced costs.

Joe: (eagerly) Look! I gotta better idea. Why don't I just throw the nuts out – put 'em in a ash can?

Eff. Ex.: Can you afford it?

Joe: Sure. All I got is about 50 bags of peanuts – cost about three bucks – so I lost $25 on the rack, but I'm outa this nasty business and no more grief.

Eff. Ex.: (shaking head) Joe, it isn't quite that simple. You are in the peanut business! The minute you throw those peanuts out you are adding $1,563 of annual overhead to the rest of your operation. Joe – be realistic – can you afford to do that?

Joe: (completely crushed) It's unbelievable! Last week I was a make money. Now I'm in a trouble – justa because I think peanuts on a counter is a gonna bring me some extra profit – justa because I believe 50 bags of peanuts a week is a easy.

Eff. Ex.: (with raised eyebrow) That is the object of modern cost studies, Joe – to dispel those false illusions.

(The original source of this fable is unknown. This version is reprinted with permission from R.M.S. Wilson (1981): *Financial Dimensions of Marketing*, London: Macmillan, Vol. 1, pp. 240–242.)

CASE STUDY 2

XYZ Ltd

This example deals with the design of a distribution system.

Whatever the system adopted, it must facilitate the delivery of goods to the company's customers in usable and saleable condition. This requires that they be undamaged, arrive at the specified time and place, and in the right quantities. These requirements are not so simple to meet as they may appear: inadequate packaging, incorrect loading procedures, rough handling in transit and similar matters all hinder their attainment.

The system that is eventually specified will consist of a unique physical distribution network based on decisions on transport, warehousing, inventory management, administration and the level of service to be provided. The total system's cost is given by the simple equation:

$$D = T + FW + VW + S$$

where D = total distribution cost,
T = total transportation cost,
FW = fixed warehousing cost,
VW = variable warehousing cost (including inventory costs),
S = cost of lost sales due to either stock-outs or average delivery delay.

Each alternative system should be costed and evaluated by using this equation before the best one can be selected. This example below should help to clarify the approach that should be adopted.

XYZ Ltd has a national distribution system via six warehouses selling to wholesale customers. Ninety-five per cent of orders are delivered within 24 hours of receipt. Some figures from the last financial year are:

Sales	£5 million
Net profit (after tax)	£250,000
Finished goods inventory (average) at factory	£750,000
Finished goods inventory (average) at warehouses	£1 million

There is only one factory and this works on the basis of maximum–minimum levels of finished goods inventory to maintain the 95 per cent level of service. Each warehouse orders weekly from the factory, with special interim orders being placed for urgent requirements. Warehouse inventory levels are based on lead times of 2 to 12 days from the factory.

The marketing director is interested in the effect on costs of eliminating the warehouses and using outside carriers to make direct deliveries to customers. The estimated effects for the next year are given in Figure 1 on p. 145. On the basis of these figures it appears that the present system is least expensive. But all the relevant costs have not been considered.

It is assumed that both alternatives are based on a 95 per cent level of service, so the cost of lost sales will be the same in each case and can thus be ignored for comparative purposes. However, to maintain this level of service under the existing system involves an investment of £1 million in warehouse stocks. The cost of carrying this stock is:

Cost of capital	15%
Excess handling	2%
Obsolescence	8%
Deterioration	2%
Administration	1%
	28%

(This figure of 28 per cent excludes an allowance for the risks of price changes, variable markets, etc., which would make it even higher.)

		Shipments to warehouses	Shipments to customers
Transport:	To warehouses	£150,000	
	Local	37,500	
	Direct		330,000
Warehousing:	Rent	52,500	2,500
	Salaries	65,000	20,000
	Insurance	17,500	10,000
	Rates	7,500	5,000
	Other	15,000	5,000
	Communications	22,500	30,000
Total distribution costs		£367,500	£402,400

Figure 1

Thus 28 per cent of £1 million is £280,000 which is the amount saved by adopting the proposed alternative of direct delivery, and shows that this is, in fact, the better choice. Further savings could also be made in manufacturing costs as a result of producing for one central inventory rather than for a central inventory plus six warehouses.

The above example shows the need to consider the total situation, not merely segments of it. A variation would have been to consider the financial alternatives of owning or leasing the warehouses. The leasing alternative provides greater flexibility and less risk unless volume is large and demand stable. This is so because the cost of storage should be related to the average area (i.e. the number of square metres) in use per period, and leasing charges will be proportional to this area whereas fixed ownership costs remain the same regardless of usage.

Cost–volume analysis can be used to aid the decision maker faced with such choices as:

1. leasing or buying premises;
2. leasing or owning vehicles;
3. using agents or setting up branch offices.

In the case of warehousing Figure 2 summarizes the situation, showing the storage space at which ownership costs are identical with leasing charges (B). At greater volume requirements ownership is cheaper, and at lesser volumes leasing is to be preferred.

CASE STUDY 3

WFC Ltd

The following example illustrates the importance of accurate forecasts of cash flows (representing sales value, cost of sales, operating costs and initial

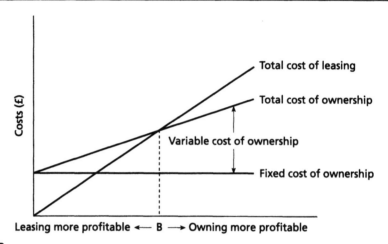

Figure 2

investment). Taxation is deliberately ignored. (The example is adapted from Winer (1966).)

A proposal has been put forward in the form of a marketing plan to launch a new line of toys. Cash-flow forecasts are shown in Figure 3. Note that depreciation is not, in fact, a cash cost. It is shown here simply as a footnote to indicate that there will be no cash inflow at the end of Year 5 from the sale of the equipment since that equipment is not expected to have any residual value at that point in time.

Proposal	Add a new line of toys.
Cash investment (£'000s)	
Production equipment	1,000
Recruiting and training sales staff	100
Promotional material	10
Inventory and debtors	190
	1,300
Projected sales volume (£'000s)	
Year 1	600
Year 2	1,000
Year 3	1,200
Year 4	1,000
Year 5 (final year)	800
Cost of sales	30% of sales value
Direct operating costs	£100,000 per annum
Depreciation of equipment	£200,000 per annum. No salvage value.

Figure 3

The evaluation of the plan is shown in Figure 4 which is largely self-explanatory. Cost of capital is shown as being 18 per cent. This can be taken to be the minimum required rate of return from the plan (thus reflecting equivalent returns from alternative plans of comparable risk). The plan's net present value is £447,000 which results when the discounted inflows and outflows are summed and the initial investment deducted from the total:

Total discounted value of inflows and outflows from Year 1 to Year 5	£1,747,000
Initial investment	£1,300,000
Net present value	£ 447,000

From these figures it is also possible to calculate the PV index:

$$\frac{£1,747,000}{£1,300,000} = 1.34$$

In other words, the plan promises to generate £1.34 for every £1.00 invested in it, expressed in terms of current £s. Since the PV index exceeds unity, hence the NPV is positive, the plan appears to be economically viable. However, various additional questions need to be raised, such as:

- Is there sufficient funding available to meet the initial investment requirements of £1,300,000?
- Can the plan be modified to earn even more than £1.34 per £1.00 of investment?
- Are there alternatives available that may be more attractive?
- How sensitive is the plan's NPV to changes in flow estimates, including their timing?

From the data given in Figure 4 it is possible to calculate the payback period of the plan and the accounting rate of return, as follows.

(£'000s)		Year				
	0	1	2	3	4	5
1 Cash investment	(1,300)					
2 Sales revenue		600	1,000	1,200	1,000	800
3 Cost of sales		(180)	(300)	(360)	(300)	(240)
4 Operating costs		(100)	(100)	(100)	(100)	(100)
5 Recovery of investment in inventory and debtors						190
6 Cash flows	(1,300)	320	600	740	600	650
7 Discount factor at 18%	1.00	0.847	0.718	0.609	0.516	0.437
8 Discounted cash flow	(1,300)	271	431	451	310	284
9 NPV	447					

Figure 4

Payback period is the length of time it takes to recover the initial investment.

		£'000s
	Year 1	320
	Year 2	600
380/740	Year 3	380
		1,300

It will be 2 years and 187 days (assuming an even pattern of inflows). The investment is exposed, therefore, over half of the anticipated life of the plan.

The accounting rate of return is an accounting (rather than cash flow) measure of the average profitability of the plan.

Average profits will be (in £'000s):

$$\frac{£(320 + 600 + 740 + 600 + 460)}{5} - £200$$

$$\frac{£2,720}{5} - £200 = £344$$

It is necessary to deduct depreciation as an expense in calculating the average accounting profit.

Average investment will be (in £'000s)

$$\frac{£1,300 - £190}{2} = £555$$

The ARR (accounting, or average, rate of return) will be:

$$\frac{£344}{£555} \times 100 = 62\%$$

CASE STUDY 4

Sales operations

A major aid in controlling selling costs is to personalize them: if salespeople know that all the costs they incur will be recorded against their budgets, they will tend to be more cost-conscious. Control is not facilitated by the averaging of such costs (e.g. entertaining, samples, travelling, telephone, stationery, etc.) over products sold.

Attention should not be drawn narrowly towards cost minimization but the aim should be to get better returns from the available resources. Sales personnel should be directed towards increasing their sales activity per hour and to pushing the most profitable lines. Profit contribution will be the ultimate measure of sales success rather than cost minimization, and this means that salespeople should avoid spending large amounts on entertaining and travel for small orders, quoting unrealistic prices, promising impossible delivery dates, creating confusion that leads to administrative difficulties, or maximizing sales volume (as so often happens) regardless of profit contribution. A high level of sales volume does not necessarily carry with it an increasing rate of profitability. It follows, therefore, that sales effort should be directed towards those customers who have the greatest profit potential. If sales managers focus their attention exclusively on expense reports, the result may well be that a high level of efficiency is achieved, but if no attention is paid to the allocation of effort it may prove to be the case that the level of effectiveness is low (e.g. through servicing a large number of small accounts).

The preoccupation with sales volume that is found amongst sales personnel may cause an order for £10,000 to be viewed as being better than an order for £5,000 despite the fact that the former may be only half as profitable as the latter (or may have taken five times as long to secure). Similarly, a preoccupation with gross margins may cause 150 orders of £100 each with a 25 per cent margin to be viewed more favourably than an order of £1,000,000 with a 1 per cent margin. The cost of processing an order for £1 is unlikely to differ from the cost of processing an order for £1,000,000 but apart from not knowing the cost of processing orders, relatively few companies know the profitability of different orders, or of different accounts. It has been suggested that 50–75 per cent of customers in most instances contribute to losses rather than to profits, so each account should be analysed to see if it makes a positive contribution. An easy way to do this is shown in Figure 5.

This simple method of computing the contribution made by different accounts is easy to apply and can readily show those that are incurring higher costs than the revenue they produce. A fuller analysis can be carried out within the framework of Figure 6. Customer analysis of this type enables relative profit contributions and the distribution of marketing effort to be attached to order-size groups. The outcome is a

Annual salary per salesperson	£7,000	
Average expenses (including car)	£6,200	
Total cost	£13,200	
Number of days spent selling	220	
Cost per day	£60	
Average calls per day	5	
Average cost per call	£12	

	Sales account A	Sales account B
Annual sales volume	£1,600	£4,800
Sales calls per year	6	8
Cost per call	£12	£12
Total call cost	£72	£96
Commission rate	5%	5%
Commission paid	£80	£240
Account profit (loss)	£(28)	£96

Figure 5 Account contributions

Customer volume group; amount of annual purchases (£)	Number of accounts percentage of total	Number of calls percentage of total	Sales percentage of total	Gross profit percentage of total	Selling expenses percentage of sales	Operating profit percentage of sales
0–5						
6–10						
11–25						
26–50						
51–100						
101–150						
151–200						
201–250						
251–300						
301–400						
401–500						
501–750						
751–1000						
Over 1000						
No sales			—	—	—	—
Total of averages	100.00	100.00	100.00			

Figure 6

most straightforward schedule of profitable versus unprofitable order-size groups, and these can be investigated further to see if any particular order-size group contains a preponderance of specific customer types. If so, the management must decide if it can make these groups more profitable, if it should stop selling to them, or what other course of action may be appropriate.

From top management's point of view, the information that is required on the financial dimensions of sales operations consists of:

1. the contribution from sales and its comparison with the requirements of the budget;
2. the extent to which variances have arisen from changes in the volume of sales, the varying of sales margins, or the mix of products sold;
3. the extent of cost variances;
4. the volume of orders placed for future delivery in relation to available productive capacity.

This information is essential (and in itself sufficient) to indicate whether the company is keeping in line with the budgeted objectives. It also shows the factors causing deviations from plan insofar as the sales function is concerned.

From this it is possible for further studies to be carried out at lower managerial levels to pinpoint and remedy basic causes.

The cost of credit

Allowance in planning and controlling cost levels should always be made for the costs of providing credit, the costs of giving cash or trade discounts and the losses due to debts' turning out to be bad. The estimating of the amounts to allow for these items will tend to be influenced by past experience, current practice and future expectations. Compare, for instance, the sale to a normal customer amounting to £1,500 in value with a sale to an occasional trade customer who expects a trade discount of 33⅓ per cent, giving a value for the same order of only £1,000. Also consider the sale of goods to the value of £1,000 on 90 days' credit terms with an average bad debt rate of 2 per cent:

Value of sale		£1,000
Interest cost: 90 days at 16 per cent p.a.	£40	
Bad debt risk: 0.02 × £1,000	£20	
Related costs		£60

In contrast, let us assume that a cash discount of 5 per cent is allowed for settlement within 14 days:

Value of sale	£1,000
Cash discount at 5 per cent	£ 50
Net sum due	£ 950

It can be seen that the cost of granting credit (ignoring the additional book-keeping and administration costs that this causes) exceeds the cost of a generous cash discount, and there is no risk of debts' turning out to be bad or of costs in extending credit when all sales are on a cash basis.

CASE STUDY 5

Company A

The following case is derived from a paper presented by Paul Walley and Mike Tayles (then of Loughborough University Business School but now at Warwick Business School and Bradford Management Centre respectively) at the Management Accounting Research Group Conference, University of Aston Management Centre, 10–11 September 1992. It is used with permission.

Case A: The influence of the market

Company A is a well-known multinational manufacturer of industrial paints. At one of its two main UK sites (site 1) a new accounting system has recently been introduced to replace a traditional system which had not been changed for some time and was not meeting the current needs of management.

The market that is served from site 1 is the drinks-can coatings market. This market is regarded as very competitive because the customer base is concentrated and the customers' requirements are very exacting. A typical customer would be a packaging company that has a contract to supply painted cans to a soft drinks manufacturer. The liaison between the can producer and its customer can be so close that it is common for them to make joint plant location decisions in order to integrate their manufacturing systems and to eliminate the transportation of cans. As a consequence of this arrangement Company A's customer has very specific delivery and quality requirements for the paint it receives. For example, cans are coated with paint at speeds of 1,000–1,200 cans per minute and at such speeds the fluid properties of the paint become critical. Company A always tests its paint at the simulated coating speed before despatch to the customer. Furthermore, for cans containing a product with an established brand image, customers regularly insist on very close tolerances of colour matching. For this type of market the frequency of orders is low, but the quantities ordered each time are usually large. Since the product is mature, there are a number of competitors for this market and competition is usually based on price.

The technology of paint production is old and well known. Paints of this type are made in a batch chemical process, whereby solid ingredients are processed and ground, and then dissolved in solvents.

Accountants responded to the increase in competition by devising a costing system that could focus upon the price competition. An accurate product cost was required and an effort needs to be made to reduce this cost to levels comparable to those of competitors. A simple look at total costs revealed that 80–90 per cent of expenses are material costs. Existing scrap allowances were reviewed and it was realized that material wastage was too high. Solvent evaporation is such a problem that profits could be increased by up to 30 per cent if this loss could be avoided. Other materials, such as expensive dyes, suffered in-process losses such as at the weighing points. It was in the company's interest to invest in better material recording systems so that material savings could be achieved, and this is taking place.

The ability to attribute other costs to the products manufactured is also important, particularly when there is a variability about these costs with different batch sizes or the equipment used. The product costing system was changed so that many of the indirect manufacturing costs that had previously been absorbed by machine time were now absorbed using other allocation bases. The system looks very much like an activity-based costing (ABC) system, but it does not have the level of the detail that is frequently observed in ABC systems. (For example, energy costs are not collected for each individual process.) The system was designed to highlight areas in which cost control is important, such as the areas where the process is more variable. For example, one major influence on batch cost variability was found to be the colour matching process. Each addition of the extra dye, or other ingredients, and the subsequent mixing, was found to be costly. A badly matched batch of paint could take three attempts to produce the correct shade and this significantly affected total batch costs. The cost system therefore used 'colour matching' as an allocation base so that the cost of this process was emphasized in the product cost. In their drive towards total quality it also gave management a useful performance measure: operators now have a chart indicating how many repeat colour matching operations they have to perform. This allocation base becomes especially important for smaller batches of paint because this cost is spread across a smaller volume of product.

A number of other benefits have accrued from this new system. The system gives an indication of the cost variation due to batch size variability, it provides better information for product scheduling purposes, and it highlights the cost of overproduction of specialized batches.

The degree of success has been enhanced by the 'ownership' of the system being held jointly by all the management team, which is due, in part, to the method of implementation of the new cost system. All of the senior management team belonged to the costing system design committee and they each had a contribution to make to the outcome. The most enthusiastic person on site was the manufacturing manager!

The management of Company A has been so pleased with the achievements on site 1 that it plans to modernize the accounting system on site 2, which satisfies a totally different market. Site 2 produces a differing variety of paints for other industrial markets. The principal product range is in the marine coatings market, where the company has a technical lead over its competitors.

One of the biggest costs for a large ship, such as an oil tanker, is the fuel it consumes. In the past ships progressively became less efficient and slower after leaving dry dock because of the ever-increasing drag as a result of barnacle encrustation on their hulls below the water line. Paints were developed, using a special additive, which prevented this encrustation because the paint slowly wore off! The first paints that came onto the market were not considered to be completely ecologically friendly, and so Company A developed a new paint, with similar properties, but which did not cause damage to sea-life, thus giving it an important competitive advantage.

The company's marketing team was quick to capitalize on the advantages that the new product offered. The new paint, when compared to traditional paints, allowed a ship to stay out of dry dock for longer, increased its fuel efficiency, and sustained the ship's maximum speed, which results in faster trips and an increase in the ship's possible workload between overhauls. Hence the product has, in marketing language, an 'economic value to the consumer' (EVC). In view of its monopolistic position, Company A was able to exploit this EVC and it successfully 'managed up' its pricing of the product. A problem in this market is its fragmentation. Ships' captains often make very quick decisions about repair and overhaul, once they have called into port. As a consequence, the sales team has to be in the right place at the right time and, with thousands of ships at sea at any one time, this is an expensive task.

Product quality requirements at this second site are very different from those at the first. Obviously, the technical performance of the paint is an important requirement, but other factors such as colour matching are rarely a worry. However, delivery speed becomes an important consideration because ships' captains want to minimize the wait in dry dock, and they do not place an order until they are in port.

An issue raised by the authors with Company A's accountants is the extent to which site 1's new system is compatible with site 2's requirements. Arguably, whilst the manufacturing process may be similar, the management tasks for site 2 are very different. Material efficiency will have an important leverage on profits in both cases but there are different sources of cost variability within the manufacturing processes. Using an analytical framework that has been derived from manufacturing theory, a comparison between important decision criteria at the two sites can be made. These are shown in Figure 7.

Discussion of Case A

This case demonstrates potential influencing factors in the design of costing systems and performance measures that result predominantly from the market place. It is not simply the *extent* of the market that influences the system's design, but the *nature* of the competition which, in turn, is determined by the chosen competitive strategy

	Site 1	*Site 2*
Market	Packaging	Marine
Demand	High volume Large orders Concentrated	Medium volume Smaller orders Fragmented
Competition	High	None directly
Order-winning criteria	Price Delivery reliability	Technical performance Delivery speed
Qualifying criteria	Delivery speed Performance Colour match	Delivery reliability Price
Key management tasks	Cost control Quality control Smooth flow Eliminate variability	Sales management Maintain technical lead

Figure 7 Case A: site comparisons

adopted by the company. Site 1 overtly has a cost leadership strategy and has designed an accounting system that can support this aim. The costing system is used to identify areas of potential cost reduction and to measure approximate performance. It is also used as a 'best guess' minimum long-run price indicator, although the management make no claims of 'true costs' for the system. The competitive strategy has a direct influence on the relative importance of the range of production management tasks. In this case low costs are achieved by material efficiency, low levels of in-process waste, minimization of overproduction, and process repeatability. The accounting system has to support the achievement of these aims.

Site 2 has different management tasks, even though the production process is very similar. The product's competitive edge is provided by its unique properties and so the company has adopted a different competitive strategy. One of the order-winning criteria is delivery speed, because of the selling to ships that are already in dry dock. The minimum total lead time can only be achieved by having a high availability of raw materials to avoid an ordering lead time, and to have low order back-log and WIP queuing time. These latter requirements will force the company to make a trade-off between throughput time and plant availability. The optimal policy will be to reduce throughput time sufficiently to create an adequate response time, which is essential, whilst minimizing where possible the total cost of additional inventory and unutilized plant. Site 2 will therefore have higher unit costs than site 1. Also, small variations in product cost will not cause site 2 to lose its competitive edge: in fact, the company could incorporate into the product price a premium for the perceived value added.

Selling costs will be different and will require different measures to attribute costs to products and to facilitate control. Site 1's sales team is based on site and will periodically travel to its small group of customers. The team's task will be to keep sales at a level that maximizes plant utilization without compromising delivery reliability. Site 2's sales effort is managed at a number of international locations. Sales costs per order will therefore be proportionately higher and a key task will be to assess the impact of sales costs from each location on profitability and cash flow. In the case of allocating selling costs to the products from site 2, it would be useful to start with the selling and marketing costs being applied to the sales made at each location and then to work back to incorporate the manufacturing costs. In site 1 the reverse, a more conventional approach, may apply.

In conclusion, it is likely that site 2's costing system will need to focus more on non-manufacturing activities because of the differences in the cost structures of the two sites. Despite the similarity of the manufacturing processes, some aspects of plant performance are probably going to be different. Therefore, it is entirely possible that different performance measures are appropriate at each site and direct comparison of the two sites is not necessarily meaningful.

Bibliography

Abell, D. F. and Hammond, J. S. (1979) *Strategic Market Planning: Problems and Analytical Approaches*, Englewood Cliffs, NJ: Prentice-Hall.

Albers, S. (1998) 'A framework for analysis of sources of profit contribution variance between actual and plan', *International Journal of Research in Marketing* 15(2): 109–22.

American Accounting Association (1972) 'Report of Committee on Cost and Profitability Analyses for Marketing', Supplement to *The Accounting Review* 47: 575–615.

American Management Association (1959) 'The marketing audit: its nature, purposes and problems', in *Analyzing and Improving Marketing Performance*, AMA Management Report Number 32, New York: AMA.

American Marketing Association (1957) 'The values and uses of distribution cost analysis', *Journal of Marketing* 21(2), April: 395–400.

Anandarajan, A. and Christopher, M. G. (1987) 'A mission approach to customer profitability analysis', *International Journal of Physical Distribution and Materials Management* 17(7): 55–68.

Anthony, R. N. (1988) *The Management Control Function*, Boston: Harvard Business School Press.

Anthony, R. N. and Reece, J. S. (1983) *Accounting: Text and Cases*, Homewood, Ill.: Irwin (Seventh Edition).

Armitage, H. M. (1987) 'The use of management accounting techniques to improve productivity analysis in distribution operations', *International Journal of Physical Distribution and Materials Management* 17(2): 40–50.

Bancroft, A. L. and Wilson, R. M. S. (1979) 'Management accounting and marketing', *Management Accounting* (CIMA) 57(11), December: 25–30.

Banks, S. (1964) *Experimentation in Marketing*, New York: McGraw-Hill.

Barrett, T. F. (1980) 'Modular database system', *International Journal of Physical Distribution and Material Management* 12(4): 135–46.

Bastable, C. W. and Bao, D. H. (1988) 'The fiction of sales-mix and sales-quantity variances', *Accounting Horizons* 2(2), June: 10–17.

Baumol, W. J. and Sevin, C. H. (1957) 'Marketing costs and mathematical programming', *Harvard Business Review* 35(5), September–October: 52–60.

Berry, D. (1977) 'Profit contribution: accounting and marketing interface', *Industrial Marketing Management* 6(2): 125–8.

Bhaskar, K. N. and Housden, R. J. W. (1985) *Accounting Information Systems and Data Processing*, London: Heinemann.

Blanchette, D. M. (1996) 'Marketing education for accountants', *Journal of Marketing Education* Spring: 37–47.

Boulding, K. E. (1956) 'General systems theory: the skeleton of science', *Management Science* 1(1), April: 197–208.

Boulding, W. and Staelin, R. (1993) 'A look on the cost side: market share and the competitive environment', *Management Science* 12(2), Spring: 144–66.

Brockner, J., Hauser, R., Birnbaum, G., Lloyd, K., Deitcher, J., Nathanson, S. and Rubin, J. Z. (1986) 'Escalation of commitment to an ineffective course of action', *Administrative Science Quarterly* 31(1), March: 109–26.

Bucklin, L. P. (1978) *Productivity in Marketing*, Chicago: American Marketing Association.

Buzzell, R. D. and Chussil, M. J. (1985) 'Managing for tomorrow', *Sloan Management Review* 26(4), Summer: 3–13.

Buzzell, R. D. and Gale, B. T. (1987) *The PIMS Principles: Linking Strategy to Performance*, New York: Free Press.

Ceccarelli, P. and Clayton, A. S. (1992) 'How to think about the shape of your business', *The PIMS letter on Business Strategy* No. 47, London: PIMS Associates.

Chakravarthy, B. S. (1986) 'Measuring strategic performance', *Strategic Management Journal* 7: 437–58.

Chebat, J.-C., Filiatrault, P., Katz, A. and Tal, S. M. (1994) 'Strategic auditing of human and financial resource allocation in marketing', *Journal of Business Research* 31: 197–208.

Christopher, W. F. (1997) 'Marketing achievement reporting: a profitability approach', *Industrial Marketing Management* 6: 149–62.

Clark, J. M. (1923) *Studies in the Economics of Overhead Costs*, Chicago: University of Chicago Press.

Clayton, A. S. and Luchs, R. (1994) 'Strategic benchmarking at ICI fibres', *Long Range Planning* 27(3), June: 54–63.

Cox, K. K. and Enis, B. M. (1969) *Experimentation for Marketing Decisions*, Scranton, Penn: Intertext.

Crissy, W. J. E., Fischer, P. M. and Mossman, F. H. (1973) 'Segmental analysis: key to marketing profitability', *MSU Business Topics* 21(2), Spring: 42–9.

Culliton, J. W. (1948) *The Management of Marketing Costs*, Boston: Division of Research, Harvard Business School.

Cushing, B. E. (1982) *Accounting Information Systems and Business Organizations*, Reading, Mass.: Addison-Wesley.

Davis, J. (1970) *Experimental Marketing*, London: Nelson.

Day, G. S. (1990) *Market Driven Strategy*, New York: Free Press.

Day, G. S. and Fahey, L. (1988) 'Valuing marketing strategies', *Journal of Marketing* 52(3), July: 45–57.

De Kluyver, C. A. and Pessemier, E. A. (1986) 'Benefits of a marketing budgeting model: two case studies', *Sloan Management Review* 28(1), Fall: 27–38.

Doyle, P. (1987) 'Marketing and the British chief executive', *Journal of Marketing Management* 3(2), Winter: 121–32.

—— (1994) *Marketing Management and Strategy*, London: Prentice-Hall.

Drucker, P. F. (1973) *Management: Tasks, Responsibilities and Practices*, New York: Harper & Row.

Duffy, M. F. (1989) 'ZBB, MBO, PPB, and their effectiveness within the planning/marketing process', *Strategic Management Journal* 10(2): 163–73.

Emmanuel, C. R., Otley, D. T. and Merchant, K. (1980) *Accounting for Management Control*, London: Chapman & Hall (Second Edition).

Farris, P. W. and Reibstein, D. J. (1979) 'How prices, expenditure and profit are linked', *Harvard Business Review* 57(6), November–December: 173–84.

Feder, R. A. (1965) 'How to measure marketing performance', *Harvard Business Review* 43(3), May–June: 132–42.

Field, G. A. and Gabhart, D. R. L. (1971) 'Cultural lag and homeostatis in accounting theory and practice', *MSU Business Topics* 19(2), Spring: 31–7.

Filiatrault, P. and Chebat, J.-C. (1987) 'Marketing budgeting practices: an empirical study', *Developments in Marketing Science* 10: 278–82.

—— (1990) 'How service firms set their marketing budgets', *Industrial Marketing Management* 19: 63–7.

Foster, G. and Gupta, M. (1994) 'Marketing, cost management and management accounting', *Journal of Management Accounting Research* 6: 43–77.

Gibson, B. (1990) 'Determining meaningful sales relational (mix) variances', *Accounting and Business Research* 21(81), Winter: 35–40.

Gilligan, C. T. and Wilson, R. M. S. (2000) *Strategic Marketing Planning*, Oxford: Butterworth-Heinemann.

Gilmour, P. (1976) 'Cost and profitability analyses for marketing', *The Australian Accountant* 46(1), January–February: 34–41.

Goodman, S. R. (1970a) *Techniques of Profitability Analysis*, New York: Wiley.

—— (1970b) *The Marketing Controller Concept: An Inquiry into Financial/Marketing Relationships in Selected Consumer Companies*, Cambridge, Mass.: Marketing Science Institute (Special Report).

Govindarajan, V. and Shank, J. K. (1989) 'Profit variance, analysis: a strategic focus', *Issues in Accounting Education* 4(2), Fall: 396–410.

Grashof, J. F. (1975) 'Conducting and using a marketing audit' in E. J. McCarthy, J. F. Grashof and A. A. Brogowicz (eds) (1975) *Readings in Basic Marketing*, Homeward, Ill.: Irwin.

Grundy, A. (1986) 'Why accountants and marketing men should be friends', *Certified Accountant* November: 12–15.

Harrison, G. L. (1978) 'The accountant's role in marketing: a bibliographic study and analysis of its origins and development', CIEBR Discussion Paper, No. 85 (General Series), Centre for Industrial, Economic and Business Research, University of Warwick.

Hirsch, M. L. (1988) *Advanced Management Accounting*, Boston: PWS-Kent.

Hise, R. T. and Strawser, R. H. (1970) 'Application of budgeting techniques to marketing operations', *MSU Business Topics* 18(3), Summer: 69–75.

Hulbert, J. M. and Toy, N. E. (1977) 'A strategic framework for marketing control', *Journal of Marketing* 41(2), April: 12–20.

Ingham, H. and Harrington, L. T. (1980) *Interfirm Comparison*, London: Heinemann.

Jackson, D. W., Ostrom, L. L. and Smith, C. H. (1977) *Marketing Profitability Analysis: An Annotated Bibliography*, Chicago: American Marketing Association (Bibliography Series No. 30).

Kaplan, R. S. and Norton, D. P. (1992) 'The balanced scorecard – measures that drive performance', *Harvard Business Review* 70(1), January–February: 71–9.

—— (1993) 'Putting the balanced scorecard to work', *Harvard Business Review* 71(5), September–October.

—— (1996) *The Balanced Scorecard*, Boston: Harvard Business School Press.

Kauffman, N. L. and Sopariwala, P. R. (1995) 'Marketing share and market size variances in a multi-product environment: an evaluation of competing formulations', *Journal of Accounting Education* 13(4): 463–78.

Kirpalani, V. H. and Shapiro, S. J. (1979) *Marketing Effectiveness: Insights from Accounting and Finance – An Annotated Bibliography, 1960–77*, Chicago: American Marketing Association (Bibliography Series No. 33).

Kjaer-Hanson, M. (ed.) (1965) *Cost Problems in Modern Marketing*, Amsterdam: North-Holland.

Kotler, P. (1967) *Marketing Management: Analysis, Planning and Control*, Englewood Cliffs, NJ: Prentice-Hall (First Edition).

—— (1988) *Marketing Management: Analysis, Planning, Implementation and Control*, Englewood Cliffs, NJ: Prentice-Hall (Sixth Edition).

Kotler, P. Gregor, W. T. and Rodgers, W. H. (1989) 'The marketing audit comes of age', *Sloan Management Review* 30(2), Winter: 49–62.

Lambert, D. M. and Sterling, J. U. (1987) 'What types of profitability reports do marketing managers receive?', *Industrial Marketing Management* 16: 295–303.

Lisle, G. (ed.) (1903) *Encyclopaedia of Accounting*, Edinburgh: William Green.

Lowe, E. A. and Shaw, R. W. (1968) 'An analysis of managerial biasing: evidence from a company's budgeting process', *Journal of Management Studies* 5(3), October: 304–15.

Magrath, A. J. and Hardy, K. G. (1986) 'Cost containment in marketing', *Journal of Business Strategy* 7(2): 14–21.

Malcom, R. E. (1978) 'The effect of product aggregation in determining sales variances', *The Accounting Review* 53(1), January: 162–9.

Mehotra, S. (1984) 'How to measure marketing productivity', *Journal of Advertising Research* 24(3): 9–15.

Meldrum, M. J., Ward, K. and Srikanthan, S. (1986) 'Can you really account for marketing?', *Marketing Intelligence and Planning* 4(4): 39–45.

—— (1987) 'Needs, issues and direction in the marketing accountancy divide', *Quarterly Review of Marketing* 12(3–4): 5–12.

Mossman, F. H. and Worrell, M. L. (1966) 'Analytical methods of measuring marketing profitability: a matrix approach', *MSU Business Topics* 14(4): 35–45.

Mossman, F. H., Fischer, P. M. and Crissy, W. J. E. (1974) 'New approaches to analyzing marketing profitability', *Journal of Marketing* 38(2): 43–8.

Mossman, F. H., Crissy, W. J. E. and Fischer, P. M. (1978) *Financial Dimensions of Marketing Management*, New York: Wiley.

Murray, J. A. and O'Driscoll, A. (1996) *Strategy and Process in Marketing*, London: Prentice-Hall.

National Association of Accountants (1973) *Information for Marketing Management*, New York: NAA.

Neth, J. T. (1966) 'Program budgets for a marketing group', *Management Accounting* (IMA) 47(10), June: 8–17.

Otley, D. T. (1985) 'The accuracy of budgetary estimates: some statistical evidence', *Journal of Business Finance and Accounting* 12(3): 415–28.

Otley, D. T. and Berry, A. J. (1980) 'Control, organization and accounting', *Accounting, Organizations and Society* 5(2): 231–46.

Piercy, N. F. (1986) *Marketing Budgeting*, London: Croom Helm.

—— (1987) 'The marketing budgeting process: marketing management implications', *Journal of Marketing* 51(4), October: 45–9.

Ploos van Austel, M. J. (1987) 'Physical distribution cost control', *International Journal of Physical Distribution and Materials Management* 17(2): 67–78.

Pyne, F. G. (1984) 'Better operating statements for the marketing director', *Accountancy* 95(1086), February: 87–90.

—— (1985) 'Accountancy that helps to meet and beat competition', *Accountancy* 96(1104), August: 104–7.

Rados, D. L. (1992) *Pushing the Numbers in Marketing: A Real-World Guide to Essential Financial Analysis*, Westport, Conn.: Quorum Books.

Rathe, A. W. (1960) 'Management control in business' in D. G. Malcolm and A. J. Rowe (eds) *Management Control Systems*, New York: Wiley.

Ratnatunga, J. T. D. (1983) *Financial Controls in Marketing: The Accounting–Marketing Interface*, Canberra: Canberra College of Advanced Education.

—— (1988) *Accounting for Competitive Marketing*, London: CIMA (Occasional Paper Series).

Ratnatunga, J. T. D., Pike, R. H. and Hooley, G. J. (1988) 'The application of management accounting techniques to marketing', *Accounting and Business Research* 18(72), Autumn: 363–70.

—— (1989) 'New evidence on the accounting–marketing interface', *The British Accounting Review* 21(4), December: 351–70.

Robinson, S. J. Q., Hichens, R. E. and Wade, D. P. (1978) 'The directional policy matrix – a tool for strategic planning', *Long Range Planning* 11(3), June: 8–15.

Saunders, J. A. (1987) 'Attitudes, structure and behaviour in a successful company', *Journal of Marketing Management* 3(2): 173–83.

Schiff, M. and Lewin, A. Y. (1970) 'The impact of people on budgets', *The Accounting Review* 45(2), April: 259–68.

Schiff, M. and Mellman, M. (1962) *The Financial Management of the Marketing Function*, New York: Financial Executives Research Foundation.

Schiff, M. and Schiff, J. (1994) *Marketing Costs – Their Nature and Use in Decision Making and Performance Measurement*, Montvale, NJ: Institute of Management Accountants.

Sevin, C. H. (1965) *Marketing Productivity Analysis*, New York: McGraw-Hill.

Shank, J. K. and Churchill, N. C. (1977) 'Variance analysis: a management-oriented approach', *The Accounting Review* 52(3): 950–67.

Shapiro, S. J. and Kirpalani, V. H. (eds) (1984) *Marketing Effectiveness: Insights from Accounting and Finance*, Boston: Allyn & Bacon.

Shuchman, A. (1950) 'The marketing audit: its nature, purposes and problems', in A. R. Oxenfeldt and R. D. Crisp (eds) *Analyzing and Improving Marketing Performance*, New York: American Management Association Report No. 32.

Simmonds, K. (1970) 'Marketing and management accounting', *Management Accounting* (CIMA) 48(2), February: 41.

—— (1981a) 'Strategic management accounting', *Management Accounting* (CIMA) 59(4), April: 26–9.

—— (1981b) 'Marketing control: from sources to confluence', Foreword to Wilson (1981).

—— (1982) 'Strategic management accounting for pricing: a case example', *Accounting and Business Research* 12(47), Summer: 206–14.

—— (1985) 'How to compete', *Management Today*, August: 39–43, 84.

—— (1986) 'The accounting assessment of competitive position', *European Journal of Marketing* 20(1): 16–31.

Siu, N. Y. M. and Wilson, R. M. S. (1998) 'Modelling marketing orientation: an application in the education sector', *Journal of Marketing Management* 14(4), May: 293–323.

Srikanathan, S., Ward, K. and Meldrum, M. J. (1986) 'Reducing the costs of the marketing game', *Management Accounting* (CIMA) 64(10), November: 48–51.

—— (1987a) 'Segment profitability: a positive contribution', *Management Accounting* (CIMA) 65(4), April: 27–30.

—— (1987b) 'Marketing: the unrecognised asset', *Management Accounting* (CIMA) 65(5), May: 38–42.

Srivastava, R. K. Shervani, T. A. and Fahey, L. (1998) 'Market-based assets and shareholder value: a framework for analysis', *Journal of Marketing* 62(1), January: 2–18.

Staw, B. M. and Ross, J. (1987a) 'Knowing when to pull the plug', *Harvard Business Review* 65(2), March–April: 68–74.

—— (1987b) 'Behavior in escalation situation: antecedents, prototypes and solutions', *Research in Organizational Behavior* 9: 39–78.

Thomas, M. J. (1984) 'The meaning of marketing productivity analysis', *Marketing Intelligence and Planning* 2(2): 13–28.

—— (1986) 'Marketing productivity analysis: a research report', *Marketing Intelligence and Planning* 4(2).

Tirmann, E. A. (1971) 'Should your marketing be audited?', *European Business* Autumn: 49–56.

Trebuss, A. S. (1976) 'The marketing controller: financial support to the marketing function', *Canadian Business Review* 3, Autumn: 30–3.

Venkatesan, M. and Holloway, R. J. (1971) *An Introduction to Marketing Experimentation: Methods, Applications and Problems*, New York: Free Press.

Walley, P. and Tayles, M. E. (1992) 'Manufacturing strategy and its implications for management accounting – three case examples', paper presented at Management Accounting Research Group Conference, University of Aston Management Centre, 10–11 September.

Ward, K. (1989) *Financial Aspects of Marketing*, Oxford: Heinemann.

Westwick, C. A. (1987) *How to Use Management Ratios*, Aldershot: Gower (Second Edition).

Wiener, N. (1948) *Cybernetics*, Cambridge, Mass.: MIT Press.

Williamson, R. J. (1979) *Marketing for Accountants and Managers*, London: Heinemann.

Wills, G. S. C., Christopher, M. G. and Walters, D. W. (1972) *Output Budgeting in Marketing*, Bradford: MCB.

Wilson, A. (1982) *Marketing Audit Check Lists*, London: McGraw-Hill.

Wilson, R. M. S. (1970) 'Accounting approaches to marketing control', *Management Accounting* (CIMA) 48(2), February: 51–8.

—— (1971) 'The role of the accountant in marketing', *Marketing Forum* May–June: 21–33.

—— (1972) 'Financial control of physical distribution management: some basic considerations', *International Journal of Physical Distribution* 3(1), Autumn: 7–20.

—— (1973) *Management Controls in Marketing*, London: Heinemann.

—— (1975) 'Marketing control: a financial perspective', *The Business Graduate* 5(2), Summer: 15–20.

—— (1979) *Management Controls and Marketing Planning*, London: Heinemann.

—— (ed) (1981) *Financial Dimensions of Marketing*, London: Macmillan (2 vols).

—— (1983) *Cost Control Handbook*, Aldershot: Gower (Second Edition).

—— (1984) 'Financial control of the marketing function', Chapter 12 (pp. 130–53) in N. A. Hart (ed.) *The Marketing of Industrial Products*, London: McGraw-Hill (Second Edition).

—— (1986) 'Accounting for marketing assets', *European Journal of Marketing* 20(1): 51–74.

—— (1988) 'Marketing and the management accountant', Chapter 13 (pp. 255–295) in R. Cowe (ed.) *Handbook of Management Accounting*, Aldershot: Gower (Second Edition).

—— (1995a) 'Marketing budgeting and resource allocation', pp. 270–300 in M. J. Baker (ed.) *Companion Encyclopaedia of Marketing*, London: Routledge.

—— (1995b) 'Strategic management accounting', Chapter 8 (pp. 159–90) in D. J. Ashton, T. M. Hopper and R. W. Scapens (eds) *Issues in Management Accounting*, London: Prentice-Hall (Second Edition).

—— (1997a) 'The case for strategic control', pp. 152–81 in I. Lapsley and R. M. S. Wilson (eds) *Explorations in Financial Control*, London: International Thomson Business Press.

—— (1997b) *Strategic Cost Management*, Aldershot: Ashgate/Dartmouth.

—— (forthcoming) *Marketing Controllership*, Aldershot: Ashgate/Dartmouth.

Wilson, R. M. S. and Bancroft, A. L. (1983a) *The Application of Management Accounting Techniques to the Planning and Control of Marketing of Consumer Non-durables*, London: CIMA (Occasional Papers Series).

—— (1983b) 'Management for marketing – some industry practices', *Management Accounting* (CIMA) 61(2), February: 26–8.

Wilson, R. M. S. and Chua, W. F. (1993) *Managerial Accounting: Method and Meaning*, London: Chapman & Hall (Second Edition).

Wilson, R. M. S. and Fook, N. Y. M. (1990) 'Improving marketing orientation', *Marketing Business*, Issue 11, June: 22–3.

Wilson, R. M. S. and Gilligan, C. T. (1997) *Strategic Marketing Management: Planning, Implementation and Control*, Oxford: Butterworth-Heinemann (Second Edition).

—— (2000) *Strategic Marketing Control*, Oxford: Butterworth-Heinemann.

Wilson, R. M. S. and Zhang, Q. (1997) 'Entrapment and escalating commitment in investment decision-making: a review', *The British Accounting Review* 29(3), September: 277–305.

Winer, L. (1966) 'A profit-oriented decision system', *Journal of Marketing* 30, April: 38–44.

Index